The
Bean, Pea
& Lentil
Cookbook

The Bean, Pea & Lentil Cookbook

Maria Luisa Scott, Jack Denton Scott,
and the Editors of Consumer
Reports Books

CONSUMER REPORTS BOOKS
A Division of Consumers Union
Yonkers, New York

LIBRARY OF CONGRESS CATALOGING-IN-PUBLICATION DATA

Scott, Maria Luisa.
   The bean, pea & lentil cookbook / Maria Luisa Scott, Jack Denton Scott, and the
editors of Consumer Reports Books.
      p.   cm.
   Includes index.
   ISBN 0-89043-363-1
   1. Cookery (Beans)   2. Cookery (Peas)   3. Cookery (Lentils)   I. Scott, Jack
Denton, 1915–   .
II. Consumer Reports Books.   III. Title.
TX803.B4S37   1991
641.6′565—dc20   90-22362
                                                                      CIP
                                                                      Rev.

Design By Kathryn Parise
Fourth printing, November 1992
Fifth printing, April 1994
Manufactured in the United States of America

The Bean, Pea & Lentil Cookbook is a Consumer Reports Book published by Consumers Union, the nonprofit organization that publishes *Consumer Reports,* the monthly magazine of test reports, product Ratings, and buying guidance. Established in 1936, Consumers Union is chartered under the Not-for-Profit Corporation Law of the State of New York.

The purposes of Consumers Union, as stated in its charter, are to provide consumers with information and counsel on consumer goods and services, to give information on all matters relating to the expenditure of the family income, and to initiate and to cooperate with individual and group efforts seeking to create and maintain decent living standards.

Consumers Union derives its income solely from the sale of *Consumer Reports* and other publications. In addition, expenses of occasional public service efforts may be met, in part, by nonrestrictive, noncommercial contributions, grants, and fees. Consumers Union accepts no advertising or product samples and is not beholden in any way to any commercial interest. Its Ratings and reports are solely for the use of the readers of its publications. Neither the Ratings, nor the reports, nor any Consumers Union publications, including this book, may be used in advertising or for any commercial purpose. Consumers Union will take all steps open to it to prevent such uses of its materials, its name, or the name of *Consumer Reports.*

DEDICATION

This book is for Sarah Uman, who had the idea, and who brings to the authors the true meaning of the title executive editor— thoughtful authority that does much to give confidence to those with whom she works.

ACKNOWLEDGMENT

Gratitude to Mina Thompson, our sister and sister-in-law, for her discovery and skillful testing of the Maria and Pasquale Limoncelli family's old-world legume recipes.

❧ ❧ Contents ❧ ❧

✎ ✑ INTRODUCTION ✑ ✎

A Culinary Safari

Did we follow legumes around the world, or did legumes follow us? For five years we literally traveled around the world more than a dozen times, clocking 500,000 miles, concentrating on off-the-beaten-track places to complete a travel book, *Passport to Adventure*, and a number of magazine articles. Everywhere we went, we found legumes—one of the world's healthiest, most versatile, and most ancient of foods.

In fact, although our assignment did not require it, we often found ourselves on a sort of culinary safari, discovering unique ways in which to cook all the many varieties of the legume family.

Once, deep in India's jungles, researching a novel and a natural history article, we watched our camp cook, Joakium, prepare what he called "boily-brown" in a pot over barely glowing embers. This dish turned out to be braised breast of wild peacock with lentils (the Indians use lentils as often as we do potatoes). After simmering until tender, the peacock breast was browned in ghee, or clarified butter, then cut into serving portions and topped with the lentils.

The lentil, that glamour member of the legume clan, dates back some nine thousand years, as discovered by archeologists in various sites in the Middle East. Beans—kidney, navy, and pinto—were farmed in Central America in 5000 B.C. Four thousand years ago, fava beans were cultivated in North Africa and the Near East; favas were found in the ruins of Troy. Dried peas were also among the findings in Egyptian tombs of the Twelfth Dynasty.

When Columbus first came to the New World, the so-called common beans, about a dozen varieties that had originally been cultivated in tropical Mexico, also appeared as staples of the North American Indians, and were being farmed in Peru and Chile. Those same beans went to Europe in the sixteenth century. Chick-peas from Southwest Asia arrived in Sicily and Switzerland during prehistoric times, then appeared in countries around the Mediterranean, east to India, west to Brazil and Mexico. And we thought we had traveled? Compared to legumes, we're definitely Little League!

Today, these beans and their tasty cousins, lentils and peas, are found in most of our cupboards and freezers, although many of us underestimate their culinary value and versatility. A great discovery in good taste and nutritional benefits is locked up in all those boxes, cans, sealed jars, or plastic bags that contain dried, cooked, or frozen legumes.

The Legume Plant

What about the word *legume*? The French consider all vegetables legumes, but to most of us the word refers to leguminous plants, those belonging to the Leguminosae family with its more than ten thousand relatives. Beans, peas, and lentils are also known as "pulses" from the Latin *puls,* referring to an ancient bean porridge. The plants themselves are legendary food suppliers—they flourish even without cultivation in many environments throughout the world. Legumes, of course, do even better under cultivation and, as befits these plant friends of man, even enrich the soil in which they grow.

Legume plants, such as sweet peas, begin their flourishing with blossoms. Seeds then develop in the pods. When mature, the pods split open along the lengthwise seams. The entire pod and seeds of some immature legume plants can be eaten; string beans, "snap" beans, and snow peas are in this category.

Other immature legume plants have tough pods, so this variety must have its seeds removed and the pods discarded. In fact, with the exception of snow peas, which are eaten whole, pod and all, most legumes can be shelled and just the fresh seeds eaten. Called "shell beans," this category includes black-eyed peas, green peas, limas, cranberry beans, fava or broad beans, flageolets (actually pale green, tender, miniature kidney beans), white beans, and red and white kidney beans.

Often the seeds are dried in their pods before being shelled, or are shelled when fresh and then dried by mechanical means. This is done for preservation. The dried seeds can remain in perfect condition for a long time without spoiling; adventurers and explorers have found legumes their most valuable food for this reason. When we attempted to reach the North Pole in the Norwegian ketch *Havella,* our talented cook, Aage, kept us going on half a dozen varieties of rehydrated dried beans. Closer to home, in our Connecticut house, we once found a jar of Great Northern beans that was stored in a little-used kitchen cabinet for more than two years. As an experiment, we cooked them and they were perfect.

Nutrition

When rehydrated, drained, then cooked covered with a variety of liquids (chicken broth is a favorite), dried legume seeds double in volume, thus providing bulk to the diet, as well as excellent nutrition. This is especially important for the world's poor, because legumes provide tasty food for pennies.

Legume nutrition is an extra bonus for us all. *Fiber,* for example, is the magic word in health circles these days. Beans and their kin contain large portions of both dietary fiber for necessary intestinal bulk and water-soluble fiber, which is thought to aid the body in lowering cholesterol levels. In fact, just one cup of cooked beans provides one-half the daily fiber intake suggested by the National Cancer Institute. A serving of canned kidney beans contains 5.8 grams of total fiber, whereas highly touted oat bran has just 4.0 grams.

Dietary fiber in legumes also promotes bowel regularity, thus aiding in controlling glucose levels. This is important, for a stable blood glucose level prevents the release of excess insulin that builds fat storage. Legume fiber is also thought to aid in weight control by its propensity to hold water in the intestinal tract, which helps to delay hunger pangs and to lend a feeling of satiation.

Indeed, legumes are a near-perfect food—abundant in muscle-building protein, vitamins, and minerals—and they are completely cholesterol-free. They are also low in calories and sodium.

Protein is the leading nutrient in legumes, which are endowed with more of this valuable substance than any other plant food. (Vegetable lovers, and those individuals eager to stay healthy by eating the proper foods, please take notice!) A cup of cooked legumes supplies one-third of the total daily requirements for protein for an adult male.

Legumes, however, are an *incomplete* protein food source. They need a little assistance from amino acids in making up the deficit. So they should be eaten along with grains, barley, bulgur wheat, pasta, or small amounts of meat, fish, poultry, milk, or cheese. This does *not* mean that meat is necessary. To make legumes the complete protein food, eat bread with legume soups, for example, or combine legumes with rice or cheese.

Legumes are *low in fat,* unlike red meat, which derives 80 percent of its calories from fat, or hard cheeses, which contain 75 percent fat calories. And these fats are saturated fats—the health villains of many nutritionists. Legumes contain fats that are polyunsaturated, which is considered to assist in lowering the blood levels of cholesterol. In fact, most calories in legumes come from complex carbohydrates and starches which, unlike fats, are not connected to any long-term health risks.

Legumes also are excellent sources of vitamins and minerals, with a high level of B vitamins, such as thiamine, niacin, and B_6. One serving of cooked beans provides as much as 40 percent of the daily requirement of thiamine and B_6. Another health plus: Legumes are rich in calcium, phosphorus, potassium, and iron. One cup of lentils, for example, furnishes us with one-quarter of our recommended daily iron intake. To help the body absorb the iron, though, it is recommended that lentils be paired with foods high in vitamin C—broccoli, peppers, tomatoes, or citrus juices and fruits.

Some people mistakenly think that beans are fattening. A cup of cooked lentils has just 212 of the right kind of calories, while 3 ounces of hamburger has 243 and a 2-ounce piece of Cheddar cheese has 225 calories—all the wrong kind of calories, too. So replacing animal fats with legumes helps to reduce the intake of possibly damaging saturated fats and cholesterol in the diet.

Preparing and Serving Legumes

A simple variety of cooking techniques can bring beans, peas, and lentils to the height of culinary artistry—from the renowned classic dishes to the tried-and-true "peasant" offerings. As someone once said, "To cook like a peasant is to eat like a king." With their remarkable alchemy, the bland dried seeds, when simmered in liquids, absorb and produce complex and subtle favors. We ourselves have often marveled at the many delicious legume combinations we have found in our travels around the world.

Many chefs in the United States today are serving lentils, for example, as a unique and appealing base for everything from chicken to fish and various types of sausages. It's a worthy effort to give one of our oldest and most common legumes a "new" upscale identity. But legumes have been around so long that there is little to discover or rediscover about them—the Italians, for example, have long considered lentils combined with cotechino, a spicy sausage, to be a national culinary treasure. In fact, professional chefs and serious cooks worldwide have long been aware of the subtle power of legumes, not only the dried versions, but the fresh ones as well, which offer superb flavors.

Our design in this legume cookbook is to forever banish dullness from your everyday dining. We do this with the assistance of our friend and mentor, Antoine Gilly. We worked for more than a decade with him, at the time one of the four greatest living French chefs. Antoine Gilly not only has been executive chef in several of France's most prestigious restaurants, but also has cooked for King George V of England, the Prince of Wales, and Prime Minister Lloyd George. He also designed and initiated the recipes for the famous French Blue Train. As professional writers, we collaborated with him on *Antoine Gilly's Feast of France,* a much-lauded cookbook.

Antoine instructed us in everything, from the proper French-needle system of trussing a chicken to the delicate task of boning a tiny quail. It was he who first sharpened our respect for beans, peas, and lentils. For example, Gilly never served a regal-looking whole poached salmon without adding what he called its "gleaming necklace" of freshly picked sweet peas.

Antoine considered cooking with legumes to be "fun," and never tired of pointing out and demonstrating their affinity for inexpensive meats, fish, vegetables, and spices. He cooked and served them with lamb shanks, calf's tongue, pork butts, tripe, codfish, chicken, and sausages. He also liked serving lentils as a dramatic accompaniment to meat and fish, and combined them with onions or shallots, garlic, leeks, and tomatoes. More than twenty years ago he used lentils as a base for elegant offerings of pheasant breast and squab. In his honor, we offer in this book one of his most splendid recipes—the bean-based cassoulet.

Antoine Gilly considered beans, lentils, and peas to be major foods, without which no professional chef could properly function. We hope to instill this same admiration and respect for legumes in our readers. Once again, legumes have come of age to help us in our kitchens, to enhance our dining, and to promote our good health—offering us a food to live by.

A FINAL NOTE

Realizing that a majority of couples today work outside the home, we have provided in this book a variety of recipes that make for quick and easy cooking. We suggest trying some of the speedy recipes that call for using canned or frozen legumes, for example. Or you can seek out those recipes that employ quick preparation of fresh or dried legumes.

Some of the main-course dishes and classics might be considered weekend "specials," for they do require a little more effort and time. But all the recipes in this book have been carefully chosen and, we think, offer a rewarding culinary experience. Each one gives pleasure in the doing and the dining.

1

Legume Techniques, Tips, and Identification

TIMING

Professional chefs, especially those with formal training, do not specify preparation times in their recipes and declare that there is no professional hard-and-fast rule for exact cooking times of dishes, except in dessert baking, where timing is crucial. The reasons are obvious: All cooks have a different temperament—fast or slow, efficient or nonefficient—so the personality factor must be an integral part of any meal preparation time.

Cooking times, of course, are always supplied as a guide, but the pros always specify "or cook until tender." That's the true cooking key. Reasons: All foods vary in quality and freshness, which make cooking times variable at best; heating temperatures also differ (gas *vs.* electric) and ovens vary in their heating efficiency, some as much as fifty degrees or more. If your oven hasn't been calibrated recently, the timing in recipes could be thrown off, especially if precise times are suggested.

Thus, the reader should be aware that, although we state desirable cooking times in this book, as well as preheating temperatures for oven cooking, we also often make a point of restating the rule of the professionals—the sensible "or cook until tender." This dictum may mean crisp-tender or soft, or whatever the desired stage may be.

FROZEN, CANNED, OR FRESH?

Several years ago we wrote an article on canned foods that necessitated contacting several food scientists. We found, to our surprise, that canned foods have the same food value as fresh or frozen. The taste may not be the same, although that is not always the case with beans.

We offer canned-legume recipes in this book that are delicious and can be ready in minutes. Even if "fancied up" by mashing, puréeing, or in combination with other foods, canned legumes are quick and easy and may prove to be the ultimate convenience food.

Frozen legumes run a close second in the speed department, and may be somewhat superior in flavor to canned. They need no special handling—simply follow the package directions, and add spices or herbs according to your preference.

Fresh legumes, although not always available, are, in our opinion, the ultimate in flavor. They, too, need no special handling other than our recipe instructions.

Canned and dried legumes, however, do require a few special preparation techniques.

CANNED BEANS

Plain canned beans are not a food of last resort, as some people think. If handled properly, they can be excellent. When we refer to canned beans, however, we do not mean *prepared* beans—beans with salt pork, "homestyle" baked beans, and so forth. We do mean the classic varieties of canned beans on the market that have been simply cooked, with a minimum of ingredients.

Preparing canned beans is simplicity itself. Open the can, drain the beans in a colander, and rinse them thoroughly with fresh cold water. Drain well. This is done to remove any faint taste of the can itself, and to accentuate the natural flavor of the beans. Also, such rinsing does away with most of the so-called gas-causing substances.

The Question of Gas. Beans do contain some gas-causing substances, but so do seeds, nuts, melons, grapes, broccoli, cabbage, cauliflower, turnips, and numerous other vegetables and fruits. Eating beans regularly evidently lessens the tendency to flatulence; we have enjoyed beans since childhood and have never experienced any digestive disturbances.

So why label beans as the main villain, especially when scientists at the U.S. Department of Agriculture have discovered that 80 percent of the elements in beans that spark some flatulence are soluble in water? Perhaps another reason we have never had any difficulty is because we follow the custom of our father (and father-in-law), Pasquale Limoncelli, a bean epicure who always changed the soaking water three times, drained it, and again covered the beans to the top with fresh cold water. After the beans have soaked in this changed water, perhaps overnight, he drained and rinsed them again in fresh cold water. (A very important bean fact: Never cook the beans in the water in which they have soaked.)

SOAKING DRIED LEGUMES

First you have to buy the dried legumes. How can you determine the quality of packaged dried legumes without first opening the package? The plastic see-through packaging helps: The color of good dried beans and peas should be bright and "new"-looking. A dull and lackluster appearance indicates long storage. This means longer cooking, but the quality should still be acceptable.

Dried legumes should also be uniform in size, otherwise the cooking becomes complicated—the smaller legumes cook faster than the larger ones. Low quality also is indicated if the seed coats are cracked, if there appears to be an excess of foreign material in the package, or if the legumes show signs of insect damage, such as pinholes.

Thus all dried legumes need inspection or "picking over," especially those bought loose from bins. A package of loose dried legumes may include bits of dried soil, weed seeds, tiny stones, all of which are difficult for the processor to remove mechanically. We dump the raw legumes on a wide layer of white paper towels in order to highlight any residual foreign matter and then carefully remove it. It's not a particularly fast method, but it is as sure as your vision. After selecting the good dried legumes, rinse them well and drain.

The next stage is to soak the dried whole beans and peas in fresh cool water. Reason: The dried skins are so impermeable, virtually iron-clad, that water can only enter through the *helium,* that juncture where the bean or pea was once attached to its pod.

This soaking process, called *rehydration,* brings moisture back to the flesh of the bean or pea that was lost through drying. Rehydration is usually a slow process, but it ensures that the beans and peas will cook evenly and become soft, tender, and flavorful. In our experience, proper presoaking of dried legumes shortens the cooking time, thereby saving energy, and gives the legumes improved flavor, texture, appearance, and digestibility.

Remember, the soaking water should always be discarded, the legumes rinsed in fresh cold water, drained, and then cooked in more fresh cold water or the liquid of your choice. (Discarding the soaking water, contrary to some beliefs, means only a minimal loss of essential nutrients.)

Caution: Do not rinse the legumes and then hold them for a considerable period before soaking, because damp legumes run the risk of souring.

Traditional Soaking. Add 6 cups of fresh cold water for every pound of dried beans or peas and let stand at room temperature overnight. We prefer to let the beans soak for 12 hours (our first choice) or 8 hours (second choice). Make sure the container is large enough to allow the beans or peas to expand 2½ times. *Never* use hot water when soaking, because it may spoil the legumes by rushing the soaking process. Do not refrigerate soaking legumes because the water uptake will be slowed.

Quick Soaking. If you decide to press some dried beans or peas into service faster than 12 or 8 hours, this method works. Add 6 cups of fresh cold water to every pound of dried legumes. Bring *slowly* to a boil. (A quick boil over high heat risks breaking the legume skins.) Let the legumes boil slowly for 2 or 3 minutes (we prefer 3). Cover pot, remove from heat, and let stand for 1 to 2 hours. We prefer the 2-hour period. Discard the soaking water, rinse the legumes well in fresh cold water, drain well, then proceed with the recipe.

LEGUME POTPOURRI

When are beans (or lentils or peas) properly cooked? As we've stated in the beginning of this section, the taste or touch test is the surest way to know. Squeeze a few of the cooked beans lightly, or lightly prick with a fork. Correctly cooked, the beans will appear plump and soft yet still hold their shape. Overcooking makes mushy beans. So touch-test!

* * *

A 1-pound package of dry legumes produces 2 cups dry or 5 to 6 cups cooked. One cup of dried legumes produces 2½ to 3 cups cooked. One 15- or 16-ounce can of beans, drained and rinsed, produces 1⅝ cups of cooked beans.

* * *

Remember, always cover and simmer legumes. Slow-cooking keeps the skins intact and ensures tenderness.

* * *

Cooking time quick check: 45 minutes slow-cooking for fresh baby limas, to 1½ to 2 hours for Great Northern and pintos.

* * *

For salads, make sure beans, lentils, and peas are hot when mixed with the dressing, for better penetration and flavoring.

* * *

If you have difficulty locating the legumes of your choice in supermarkets, try health- or natural-food stores.

* * *

Can legumes be cooked ahead and then stored? Yes. Cook, drain well, and store well covered for up to 4 days in the refrigerator. Mixed or tossed with olive oil, tomato sauce, or seasonings, the beans are then ready to heat and to serve for a quick meal or side dish.

* * *

It's not necessary to skim foam from dried beans as they cook. Just add 1 tablespoon vegetable oil to the simmering water.

* * *

Weighty problem solved quickly: Dried beans double in volume after soaking and cooking.

* * *

We often thicken sauces by mashing a small quantity of cooked beans very well and then blending them into the sauce.

* * *

Do save liquid from beans that have been long-simmered; it makes a very tasty base for a variety of soups.

STOCKS AND BROTH

As a number of the recipes in this book call for chicken broth, it is appropriate here to point out the difference between "broth" and "stock" and to offer our recipe.

"Stock" is the simpler, weaker preparation—actually water given some authority by being simmered with vegetables and/or meat and bones. It is not reduced, so it is too bland to be used by itself, but it's excellent for braising, poaching, or used as a base for soups or stews.

Stock becomes "broth" when it is given strength of character by being reduced by half. Some chefs even add more fresh bones and vegetables after it is cooked and reduced, which gives it even greater flavor. We don't think that extra step is necessary.

A number of good commercial chicken broths are on the market, but there is nothing like your own, simmered until it is as rich as you like it, then strained and used or frozen. Some of the broth can be frozen together with nuggets of chicken meat to produce any number of future quick, delicious soups.

Chicken Broth

4 pounds chicken backs, wings, and necks
4 quarts of water
2 medium-sized onions, each stuck with 2 whole cloves
2 large celery stalks with leaves, coarsely chopped
3 medium-sized carrots, scraped and coarsely chopped
6 sprigs broad-leaf parsley
2 small bay leaves
¼ teaspoon dried thyme
8 black peppercorns, slightly crushed
1 teaspoon salt

1. Place all ingredients in a large soup pot. Cover and bring to a boil. Reduce heat to low and simmer for 30 minutes, skimming surface scum off as necessary.
2. Remove the cover and, at a bare simmer, cook for 2 hours, or until the liquid is reduced by half. Taste for seasoning.
3. Discard all vegetables, saving the chicken meat for soups. Strain the broth into a large bowl. Store in the refrigerator overnight. Sediment will settle to the bottom and fat will solidify on top.
4. Carefully remove the fat and discard it. Spoon the clear, jellied broth remaining into another bowl. Discard the sediment remaining in the first large bowl.

Makes about 2 quarts.

Legume Identification

It would be self-defeating to describe here such esoteric legumes as adzuki beans, pigeon peas, split black or golden grams, brown beans (Swedish beans), winged beans, tepari beans. We include recipes in this book only for those legumes that are easily available in supermarkets or, in a couple of instances, in natural-food shops.

Shape determines the categories of legumes: Beans are oval or kidney-shaped; lentils disklike or flattened; peas are round. *Exception:* Black-eyed peas are beanlike and elongated, even called "black-eyed beans" in some areas.

All lentils belong to one clan or species. Beans and peas, however, are members of several different species, with beans the most clannish of all. Many of the so-called common beans are members of a single species, although they come in different colors and some also have several names.

The brief descriptions and handling instructions that follow are for your convenience and serve as a "quick-check" list. (Complete soaking and cooking procedures precede this section.) All legume recipes, however, are not created equal. Some regional cooks use their own tried-and-true methods of soaking or not soaking beans. For example, in our pink bean recipe—"Mexico City Pink Beans"—the beans are simply simmered without soaking, a method often practiced by the Mexicans themselves, as we have observed in their kitchens. Also, there may be other recipes that we have collected and used from our travels that don't exactly conform to the soaking-and-cooking directions suggested here or in the preceding section. However, as a general guide, the presoaking (or quick-soaking) procedures that we have described in most of the recipes in this book are still the surest way to tenderize beans.

One bonus value of dried legumes is their long shelf life. Nevertheless, try to purchase products that are dated, so you can avoid using any that are more than a year old. As dried legumes age, they harden and darken and require longer cooking. If too old, they become so overdry that they often disintegrate in the cooking. We did, as mentioned previously, cook some overaged white beans that we had stored and forgotten, and they turned out all right. But cooking old legumes (unless out of necessity) is chancy. No health factor is involved, it's just that the legumes will not be at their best.

All the following information (with the exception of flageolets) refers to the dried variety; these are the most popular, inexpensive, and most widely available legumes nationwide. As stated previously, fresh legumes from your own garden (the best!) or from supermarkets need no description or special instructions other than those found in our recipes.

TYPES OF BEANS

Black Beans. Also known as turtle beans, and sometimes called by the Spanish *frijoles negros*. Shiny black and South American in origin, widely used in soups and rice dishes. Mealy texture, with a somewhat earthy, slight mushroom flavor. Soak in fresh cold water overnight, or for 8 hours. (Or quick-soak for 1 to 2 hours.) Drain. Cover with fresh water and bring to a boil for 10 minutes. Cover, reduce heat, and simmer for 1 to 1½ hours, or until just tender.

Cranberry Beans. Beige markings on pink skin, thus the name. Become an attractive pink when cooked. Mealy texture, nutlike flavor. Not available everywhere, but becoming more popular, and decidedly worth finding. Soak in fresh water overnight, or for 8 hours. (Or quick-soak for 1 to 2 hours.) Drain. Cover with fresh water and bring to a boil. Cover, reduce heat, and simmer for 1½ to 2 hours, or until tender.

Fava Beans. Also called broad beans. Strong personality, just this side of bitter. Texture is somewhat granular, flavor "earthy." Soak in fresh water overnight, or for 8 hours. (Or quick-soak for 1 to 2 hours.) Drain. It is important to peel off the very bitter brown skins. Boil for 10 minutes, cover, reduce heat, and simmer for 2 hours. Favas have long been favored by Italians, who prefer the young, tender, garden-fresh variety. They are often eaten raw, in salads and antipastos. (We've had dried favas in Rome, where they are simmered with onion and pork or ham.) This is a bean that can hold its own, no matter how flavorful or spicy the meat.

Navy Beans. Also called pea beans and haricot beans, which come in several varieties and colors. (Sizes, however, differ. For example, the widely used white Great Northern beans are larger than navy beans, whose secondary name *pea beans* describes their size.) Color white, mealy texture, flavor pleasant and mild. These much used, talented beans are among the leaders in picking up and passing on flavors of foods used in combination. Soak in fresh water overnight, or for 8 hours. (Or quick-soak for 1 to 2 hours.) Drain. Cover with fresh water and boil for 10 minutes. Cover, reduce heat, and simmer for 1½ to 2 hours.

Pink Beans. Pale pink, lightly touched with beige. We first discovered these beans in Peru, where they are widely used. Pink beans are also popular in Mexico, where they are sometimes interchanged with pinto beans. Mealy texture, distinct meaty flavor. Soak in fresh water overnight, or for 8 hours. Drain. (Or quick-soak for 1 to 2 hours.) Cover with fresh water and boil for 10 minutes. Cover, reduce heat, and simmer for 1½ to 2 hours.

Pinto Beans. It is not certain whether the pinto horse was named for this bean, or the bean for the horse—*pinto* is Spanish for *paint* and the pinto horse looks as if it were dabbed with paint. One version has it that Spanish explorers brought these beans to Mexico along with the first horses on this continent. Another version states that the conquistadors discovered the beans when they invaded Mexico, where the bean had been cultivated since prehistoric times (historians favor this version). Mottled with beige and brownish pink in color, these beans turn a pretty pink when cooked. They are especially popular in various versions of chili dishes. We personally prefer them to the usual kidney beans in our chili con carne. Very flavorful, mealy texture. Soak in fresh water overnight, or for 8 hours. Drain. (Or quick-soak for 1 to 2 hours.) Cover with fresh water and bring to a boil for 10 minutes. Cover, reduce heat, and simmer for 1½ to 2 hours.

Great Northern Beans. This larger ivory cousin of navy or pea beans outranks all beans in popularity. The Italians call them *cannellini*. A member of the haricot bean family, Great Northerns sometimes are called white kidney beans. They are a favorite bean in many Italian dishes, and the French also use them in their famous *cassoulet*, but sometimes use the smaller navy bean. Texture is mealy, flavor distinct but agreeably mild. Great Northern beans are democratic mixers, blending extremely well with many food combinations ranging from appetizers and purées to soups and main dishes. Soak in fresh water overnight, or for 8 hours. Drain. (Or quick-soak for 1 to 2 hours.) Cover with fresh water and boil for 10 minutes. Cover, reduce heat, and simmer for 1½ to 2 hours.

Kidney Beans. Available dark red, light red, and white, the most popular is the dark red "chili" bean, the base of the South's famous red beans and rice dish. Kidney beans rank along with Great Northern beans as America's favorite. Flavor slightly sweetish and meaty; texture is mealy. Soak in fresh water overnight, or for 8 hours. Drain. (Or quick-soak for 1 to 2 hours.) Cover with fresh water and boil for 10 minutes. Cover, reduce heat, and simmer for 1½ to 2 hours.

Lima Beans. The larger limas (especially canned) are usually called butter beans. There are two variations of limas, large and small. The large run in color from pale green or white to red, black, or mottled; the colored beans are harvested either very flat and large-veined (the flat lima), or plumpish, smaller-veined, and smaller in size (the potato lima). Another lima is a variant of the sieva or civet bean, which are small, flat limas (often called baby limas), and are white, brown, or mottled. Originating in South America, limas are the best-known legume in many parts of the world. All limas are American favorites, beginning with the American Indians who introduced us to succotash, a dish of lima beans and corn stew. Probably the most available bean in the United States, it is found either fresh, frozen, dried, or canned. A rich, starchy bean with its own distinct flavor and soft texture. Soak, covered in fresh water, overnight, or for 8 hours. (Or quick-soak for 1 to 2 hours.) Drain. Cover with fresh water and boil for 10 minutes. Cover, reduce heat, and simmer for 1 to 1½ hours.

Mung Beans. Round, small (about ¼ inch in diameter) green-golden, brown, or black. One of our oldest beans, valued by Orientals for millennia, the mung also produces the ever-popular bean sprout, long favored by the Chinese and Japanese. The mung bean itself is sweet, with an agreeably soft texture. They are not widely available except in natural-food or Oriental markets, but are a taste treat well worth the search. Cooking schools differ on their treatment of this bean: Some soak them in water for 1 hour, drain, cover with fresh water, and bring to a boil, then reduce heat and simmer for 30 minutes. Some do not soak at all, but simply simmer for 30 minutes. Your choice.

Soybeans. Despite the fact that soybeans are the most versatile of all beans and legumes, we had difficulty finding dried soybeans in markets, finally locating them in a natural-food store. It seems that most Americans currently have little use for this mild, firm-textured bean as a vegetable, even though it has more food value than any other legume and even though we found it excellent in a spicy casserole dish. The soybean is the best-kept secret of the supermarket; not many of us know that an astounding variety of table products come from this bean. Soybean oil or meal is used in the production of salads, bacon and eggs, chicken, red meats, dairy products, sauces, desserts, and fast foods. Each of us consumes approximately 5 gallons of its healthful, unsaturated golden oil each year. The United States produces about 12 billion pounds of soybean oil yearly, more than 80 percent of which is used in the food industry; the remaining 20 percent is used for industrial and export purposes.

The soybean, *glysine max,* an annual, grows to a height of 2 to 4 feet, with seeds in pods clustered about the stem. Soybeans planted from May to June produce tender, green pealike beans. These are eaten fresh in Asia and are beginning to be used in California. Soybeans also produce bean sprouts, not as tender as mung bean sprouts, but larger. The uses of soybeans are so varied they could fill this book, and include ice cream, a meat substitute or curd, *doufu* or *tofu,* and margarine. This bean, the size of a pea and colored white, black, green, or brown, although not considered a major vegetable by American cooks, deserves a high place of honor in any listing of legumes. Dried soybeans should be soaked in fresh water overnight, or for 8 hours. (Or quick-soak for 1 to 2 hours.) Drain. Cover with fresh water, bring to a boil, cover pot, reduce heat, and simmer for 2 hours or until tender.

Flageolets. The first time we had these pale green delights was in Paris, where they surrounded a beautifully roasted, juicy and pink leg of baby lamb, called a *gigot.* We have had this dish dozens of times since, always in this impressive, classic serving. The French claim to be the discoverers of flageolets, and we don't doubt it.

Flageolets are mainly available in specialty markets that offer gourmet produce, where they are usually sold fresh. Sometimes they come canned, but do try for the fresh. They are definitely worth the search. Fresh flageolets, cooked briefly, well drained, and dressed with butter or extra virgin olive oil, and lightly seasoned with salt and pepper are a decided legume taste treat. Flageolets are baby kidney beans that are taken from the pods when they are young. They rival even fresh peas in flavor, and may be the least filling of legumes. A faded emerald in their youthful coloring, the flavor is intensely fresh. They should be closely attended in the cooking and never overcooked. Test for tenderness several times, and beware of their being oversoft.

Chick-peas. With a reputation as firm as its texture, the chick-pea, one of the oldest of beans, was a favorite in ancient Rome and a long-time staple for the masses in India. The chick-pea is also a favorite today. It is superb in appetizers, soups, salads, purées, stews, and casseroles with various meats. Fortunately, the chick-pea is available everywhere dried and canned. Called *garbanzos* by Spanish-speaking people and *ceci* by Italians, the round, light tan, medium-sized bean with the nutty flavor may be the hardest and one of the heartiest of legumes. Chick-peas require long soaking and cooking. Soak them covered with fresh water overnight, or quick-soak for 2 hours. Drain. Cover with fresh water and bring to a boil. Cover, reduce heat, and simmer for 2 hours, or until tender.

Lentils. Originating in ancient Asia, it is believed that the lentil may be the oldest legume. No one, however, disagrees with the fact that the lentil is the tastiest of legumes, and many, including present-day professional chefs, consider it the classiest, using it to dress up and dignify all manner of dishes. The French especially place a high culinary value on lentils, often serving them with no dressing or seasoning other than butter.

Lentils are flat, round, and small, of a brown, green, and pink color. The light brown variety that we see most often is grown in vast quantities almost exclusively in the "Palouse," in eastern Washington State and northern Idaho, along with most of our supply of split peas. Lentils have a uniquely agreeable earthy flavor and soft texture. They do not require soaking, but do need prior sorting and rinsing. Lentils should be well-drained and then covered with fresh water. They should be brought to a boil, covered, heat reduced, then simmered for 20 minutes, or until tender. They should not be overcooked, or they become too soft, even mushy. We check for proper tenderness after 15 minutes. We also like to vary the cooking, sometimes using chicken broth and chopped onions for simmering the lentils. Even then, the saucy, delicious lentil maintains its own delicate personality. No problem at all in realizing that we are devout lentil fans!

Black-eyed Peas. A black-eyed pea looks like a large pea with a black eye, thus the name. This "pea" is actually an ancient member of the bean family, and could even be a close relative of the black mung bean. It may have originated in China, then migrated to Africa. No one seems to know exactly how this ancient bean came to Africa, but it is very popular there, and probably was first brought to our South by African slaves. This very different pea-bean also has an unusual collection of tie-in names: cornfield pea, cowpea, jerusalem pea, marble pea, and tonkin pea. Actually, the black-eyed pea is one of more than 250 variously named variants of a single species. But our black-eyed version is a pea or bean of strong character all by itself.

Cooking methods vary. Some people quick-soak them, then cook; others, because black-eyed peas have a thin skin, cook them no more than 30 minutes, checking before that time to make certain they aren't overcooked and broken up. Some recipes, depending upon what the peas are cooked with (other vegetables, meats), call for longer cooking to promote the soft melding with other foods. Southerners often combine them with rice. Available dried, also canned and frozen.

Green and Yellow Split Peas. As stated before, both of these "soup-master" peas come from a 250-by-50 mile region in eastern Washington State and northern Idaho called the "Palouse." (This word is a French variation of "green lawn," describing the gently rolling hills of the area in the spring.)

In addition to supplying the United States with 95 percent of commercial split peas and lentils, the producers of the Palouse export more than 375 million pounds of peas and lentils to nearly every region in the world, making the United States the split pea and lentil capital of the world.

It is worthwhile to note that 1 cup of the all-American split pea provides as much fiber as a small apple, and more fiber than a slice of whole wheat bread. In addition, split peas may be the world's oldest and number-one convenience food as, like all dried legumes, they require no refrigeration; split peas need no presoaking, and there is no waste at all in the cooking. Most of us use split peas in soups, and no other legume is in the same league in that regard.

This unique pea with the earthy, nutty flavor has been around since 9000 B.C. It was eaten in ancient times in India and from there was introduced into China. Dried split peas are whole garden or field peas that are field-dried, harvested, and steamed to loosen the seed coat. They are then placed in a "splitter" and the peas split at the seam. The seed coat is screened off and the pea polished before packaging or storing. Split peas require no presoaking and they cook in 30 minutes, depending upon what other foods they are simmered with.

2

Appetizers

In our travels we've discovered tempting legume hors d'oeuvres or appetizers in many places: dressed cannellini beans in Milan, hummus in Athens, and delicious purées from every corner of the globe. These appetizers are so good in themselves that they may tempt you to skip the rest of the meal.

We have included in this chapter two salads—served in smaller portions, they also make excellent appetizers.

Bean, Cheese, and Jalapeño Pepper Dip

When you need a quick appetizer for unexpected guests, here's a peppy one that has often rescued us. Serve with something cool to drink.

One 11½-ounce can condensed bean with bacon soup (do not add water)
1 tablespoon minced scallions, white part only
½ cup chopped fresh tomatoes or drained canned tomatoes
2 cups shredded Monterey Jack cheese with jalapeño peppers

1. In a saucepan, combine and blend well all ingredients.
2. Over medium heat, cook for 10 minutes, stirring often, or until the cheese is completely melted.
3. Offer as a hot dip with unsalted corn or tortilla chips. (Plenty of paper napkins, of course.)

Makes about 2½ cups.

Beans and Tuna Milanese

This dish was created in Florence, where it is called *fagioli al fiasco* (beans in a flask) because the beans are cooked by simmering them very gently in a bottle whose narrow neck prevents the escape of steam and flavor. We often use this Milanese version as an appetizer, served with warm, buttered Italian bread. The portions can also be increased for a most satisfying lunch.

    1 pound dried Great Northern beans, picked over
    5 cups homemade Chicken Broth (page 13), or canned
    3 garlic cloves, peeled and left whole
Two 7-ounce cans fancy solid albacore white tuna, drained and broken into bite-sized pieces
⅓ cup extra virgin olive oil
Juice of 1 large lemon
½ cup chopped fresh broad-leaf parsley
Salt and freshly ground black pepper to taste
6 to 8 Boston or Bibb lettuce leaves

1. Soak beans for 5 hours in water to cover; or boil in water to cover for 2 minutes, remove from heat, and let stand for 1 to 2 hours.
2. Drain the beans and place them in a large pot with enough chicken broth to cover them well. Add the garlic, bring to a boil, reduce heat, cover, and simmer *very slowly* (the broth should barely bubble over the beans) for 45 minutes, or until the beans are just tender. Do not overcook. The beans should be tender but still somewhat firm (al dente). If the liquid cooks off before the beans are tender, add small amounts of *hot* broth. Cool beans in what liquid remains.
3. Drain cooled beans and discard the garlic.
4. Add the tuna pieces, oil, lemon juice, and half the parsley. Mix carefully but well. Taste for seasoning, adding salt and pepper if needed. Add more oil or lemon juice, if desired.

5. Spoon mixture onto lettuce leaves on serving plates and sprinkle on the remaining parsley.
6. Serve with warm crusty bread.

Serves 6 to 8 as appetizer.
Serves 4 as light lunch.

Black Bean and Walnut Purée

Regardless of color, puréed beans make an excellent dipping sauce. We like this as an appetizer dip for raw vegetables.

One 16-ounce can black beans (frijoles negros in some markets)
½ teaspoon salt
⅓ cup walnuts
2 garlic cloves, peeled
⅛ teaspoon cayenne
1 small sweet red onion, peeled and minced
1 tablespoon balsamic vinegar
2 tablespoons chopped fresh broad-leaf parsley

1. Drain black beans, rinse thoroughly in cold water, and drain again.
2. Combine all ingredients in a food processor and process into a smooth purée. The mixture should not be soupy, so process carefully. Taste for seasoning.
3. Serve at room temperature with raw vegetables for dipping.

Makes approximately 2 cups.

Mexican Black Beans
"Salud!"

    2 cups dried black beans
    2 small bay leaves
    3 garlic cloves, peeled and mashed
    1 tablespoon plus ½ teaspoon salt (optional)
 1½ teaspoons olive oil
    1 tablespoon chili powder

1. Pick over beans, discarding any foreign material and imperfect beans. Rinse well.
2. Place the beans in a pot with the bay leaves and garlic. Cover with water and bring to a boil over high heat. Boil 2 minutes, remove from heat, cover, and let stand for 1 to 2 hours.
3. Return beans to medium heat, cover, and simmer for 20 minutes, or until the beans are tender and slightly chewy (al dente). Add more hot water if water cooks off. Stir in up to 2 teaspoons salt, if desired.
4. Drain beans well, discarding the bay leaf and garlic, and allow to dry at room temperature for 1 hour.
5. With the olive oil, lightly oil a saucepan. Add the dry cooked beans. Over low heat, lightly brown the beans, turning often.
6. When the beans are lightly browned and very hot, blend the chili powder with 1½ teaspoons salt and sprinkle on the beans, tossing and mixing well.
7. Serve in small warmed bowls with tortilla chips, and spoons for scooping.

Serves 6.

Toasted Black-eyed Peas

1 cup dried black-eyed peas
About 2 cups homemade Chicken Broth (page 13), or
    canned
½ teaspoon salt
⅓ cup balsamic vinegar
1 cup extra virgin olive oil
¼ teaspoon freshly ground black pepper
1 medium-sized red onion, peeled and sliced into rings
1 garlic clove, peeled and left whole
Chopped fresh broad-leaf parsley for garnish

1. Pick over peas, discarding any foreign material and imperfect beans. Rinse peas well, drain, and put in a saucepan.
2. Add enough chicken broth to cover the peas by 1 inch. Add the salt and bring broth to a boil. Boil 2 minutes, remove from heat, and soak 1 hour. Return to low heat and simmer, covered, for 30 minutes, or until the peas are tender but still intact. Drain.
3. In a bowl large enough to hold all ingredients, combine the vinegar, oil, and pepper and blend well with a whisk or beater.
4. Add the peas, onion rings, and garlic to the oil-vinegar bowl and blend well. Cover with plastic and refrigerate overnight or longer, stirring occasionally. Taste for seasoning. Discard garlic.
5. Just before serving, drain the peas, reserving the marinade. Transfer peas to a serving bowl. Stir in 3 or 4 tablespoons of the marinade. Sprinkle with parsley.
6. Serve with toast squares.

Serves 4 to 6.

Cranberry Beans, Chick-peas, and Red Pepper Salad

Canned legume salads offer swift preparation and excellent flavor. This version makes an inviting prologue to a meal.

One 1-pound can cranberry beans (or canned beans of your choice)
One 1-pound can chick-peas
1 large sweet red pepper, seeded, cored, and chopped
1 garlic clove, peeled and minced
⅓ cup finely chopped fresh basil

Salad Dressing

2 tablespoons freshly squeezed lemon juice
1 tablespoon balsamic vinegar
½ cup extra virgin olive oil
1 teaspoon salt, or to taste

1. Drain beans and chick-peas, rinse in cold water, and drain well again.
2. Combine the beans, chick-peas, red pepper, garlic, and basil in a bowl. Stir to blend.
3. Blend salad dressing ingredients thoroughly.
4. Add salad dressing to bean mixture and stir, blending well. Serve at room temperature, or slightly chilled.

Serves 4 to 6.

Danish-style Bean-Cheddar Sandwich

Here's a quick, satisfying appetizer or lunch that we often enjoy if we have leftover beans in the refrigerator. Or use a 16-ounce can of commercial beans. It's still tasty.

  8 slices light rye or whole-grain bread
16 ounces cooked beans, drained
  8 generous slices good aged Cheddar or Muenster cheese

1. Toast the bread lightly. Divide the beans into 8 equal portions and spoon 1 portion onto each slice of toast, making a smooth layer. Place a slice of cheese on each.
2. Place slices under broiler until the cheese just begins to bubble and melt.
3. Serve immediately. The "sandwich" can be eaten using a knife and fork.

Serves 8 as an appetizer or 4 for lunch with a salad.

Stufato of Fresh Fava Beans

The Italians have long favored fava beans in their cooking. These stewed favas were served often by our father and father-in-law, Pasquale Limoncelli, as an antipasto. You can use fresh lima beans if you prefer.

    3 pounds fresh unshelled fava beans
    2 tablespoons olive oil
    4 scallions, white part only, chopped
    1 garlic clove, peeled and minced
    1 tablespoon flour
    ¼ teaspoon dried rosemary
    ¼ teaspoon dried basil
    ⅛ teaspoon dried red pepper flakes
    Salt and freshly ground black pepper to taste
    About 1½ cups homemade Chicken Broth (page 13), or
        canned

1. Shell, then remove outer skins of favas.
2. In a deep saucepan, over medium heat, heat the olive oil. Add the scallions and garlic and cook 5 minutes, stirring, or until soft. Do not brown. Blend in the flour and cook 1 minute, stirring.
3. Add the fava beans, rosemary, basil, and red pepper flakes. Stir gently. Season with salt and pepper, and blend in just enough broth to cover beans. Simmer, covered, over low heat, for 15 minutes, or until the beans are tender, stirring occasionally.
4. Mash ¼ cup of the cooked beans in a bowl. Return mashed beans to the pan and stir them into the mixture.
5. Simmer, uncovered, over low heat, for 8 minutes, stirring occasionally. Serve in warm individual rimmed dishes, with halved slices of fresh Italian bread.

Serves 4.

Garlic-Bean Purée with Shrimp

Garlic, when it is roasted, loses its assertive personality and becomes mild and nutty. Put the roasted garlic in a bean purée and accompany it with shrimp, and you have an unusual and savory appetizer.

  1   large head (*not* a clove) garlic
1½   teaspoons olive oil
Two 16-ounce cans white kidney beans, drained, rinsed, and drained again
One 7-ounce jar pimientos, drained, and dried with paper towels
  1   tablespoon freshly squeezed lemon juice
  2   teaspoons tomato sauce
  3   tablespoons extra virgin olive oil
12   medium-sized shrimp, peeled, deveined, boiled in lightly salted water just until pink, and drained
Toast points for garnish

1. Cut about ½ inch from the top of the garlic head. Place head in small baking pan and drizzle with 1½ teaspoons olive oil. Completely wrap head in aluminum foil and bake in a preheated 350 F oven 1 hour, or until soft (the cloves will begin to pop out of their skins). Remove head from oven and cool. Squeeze the garlic out of skins.
2. Place garlic, beans, pimientos, lemon juice, and tomato sauce in a food processor or blender and process just until smooth and velvety, not liquidy. Leave in blender or food processor.
3. With motor running, add the 3 tablespoons of extra virgin olive oil just until blended with the bean purée.
4. Spoon purée onto individual plates, and top each portion with 3 shrimp. Garnish with toast points.

Serves 4.

Green Shrimp Toasts

Sweet, flavorful peas, one of the few foods that can hold its own in a flavor contest with shrimp, make this an appealing appetizer.

> 1 cup Purée of Green Peas (page 106)
> 1 cup minced cooked shrimp
> 1 tablespoon minced fresh dill, or 1 teaspoon dried
> Salt and freshly ground black pepper to taste
> 36 small squares toasted bread

1. Combine all ingredients except the toast squares and blend well. Taste for seasoning.
2. Spread 2 teaspoons of mixture on each toast square, arrange squares on a baking sheet, and place on the top rack in oven to broil until slightly browned. Watch carefully to make sure squares do not burn. Or set oven to highest setting and bake squares until heated through, about 3 minutes.

Makes about 2 cups spread, for 3 dozen canapés.

Hummus Bi Tahini
(Chick-pea Dip)

This is a good dip for raw vegetables and/or pieces of pita bread. It's tasty even without the sesame paste, although that addition makes it a classic.

3 cups canned chick-peas, drained, rinsed, and drained again
¼ cup sesame paste (tahini), found in specialty stores
2 tablespoons water
¼ cup strained freshly squeezed lemon juice
¼ cup extra virgin olive oil
2 garlic cloves, peeled and chopped
¼ teaspoon salt
Freshly ground black pepper to taste
½ cup chopped fresh parsley

1. In the bowl of a food processor or blender, combine the chick-peas, sesame paste, water, lemon juice, olive oil, and garlic. Process or blend until smooth and creamy in texture. Scrape down sides of bowl if necessary.
2. Add salt and pepper and process for a few seconds.
3. Taste for seasoning, adding more salt, pepper, or lemon juice to taste. If too thick, add small amounts of lemon juice and olive oil.
4. Stir in the parsley. Transfer to a bowl and refrigerate until ready to serve. Stir just before serving.

Makes about 3½ cups.

Pickled Beans with Dill

2 pounds green or yellow string beans, trimmed but left whole
1 teaspoon dried red pepper flakes
4 garlic cloves, peeled and left whole
4 large heads fresh dill, or 4 teaspoons dried
2 cups water
¼ cup salt
1 pint white vinegar

1. Pack beans into 4 sterilized pint jars.
2. To each jar, add ¼ teaspoon dried red pepper flakes, 1 garlic clove, and 1 sprig fresh dill or 1 teaspoon dried dill.
3. Combine the water, salt, and vinegar in a saucepan, bring to a boil, and pour over the beans, leaving ¼ inch head space.
4. Seal jars and process 15 minutes in boiling water to cover.
5. Store jars in a cool, dark place for 3 or 4 weeks before opening.

Makes approximately 4 pints.

White Bean Spread

½ cup dried Great Northern beans
2 cups homemade Chicken Broth (page 13), or canned
1 garlic clove, peeled and minced
2 tablespoons freshly squeezed lemon juice
2 tablespoons extra virgin olive oil
¼ teaspoon paprika
Salt and freshly ground black pepper to taste
2 tablespoons finely chopped fresh parsley
Small toast squares

1. Pick over beans, removing any foreign material. Soak beans well covered with water overnight; or boil in water for 2 minutes, remove from heat, cover, and soak 1 to 2 hours. Drain.
2. Simmer beans, covered, in chicken broth for 1 hour, or until soft. If broth cooks off before beans are soft, add small amount of *hot* broth. Drain beans well and run through a food mill, or coarsely chop in a blender or food processor. Spoon into a bowl.
3. Stir in the garlic and lemon juice, blend well, then whip in the olive oil, paprika, salt, and pepper. Taste for seasoning.
4. Sprinkle with parsley. Spoon mixture over toast squares.

Makes about 1½ cups.

White Bean, Tomato, and Mozzarella Salad

You'll need fresh vine-ripened tomatoes and fresh herbs for this dish—it's a wonderfully simple summer salad that can double as an appetizer.

One 16-ounce can white cannellini beans, or other white bean
1 cup ½-inch cubes low-fat mozzarella cheese
4 medium-sized ripe tomatoes, peeled and cut into bite-sized pieces
1 tablespoon chopped fresh basil

Salad Dressing

¼ cup virgin olive oil
1½ tablespoons balsamic vinegar
Salt and freshly ground black pepper to taste
Boston or romaine lettuce leaves
1 large tomato for garnish, peeled, cut into 8 wedges

1. Drain beans, rinse with cold water, and drain again.
2. In a large bowl, combine and mix carefully the beans, cheese, tomatoes, and half the basil.
3. Whisk the salad dressing ingredients together in a small bowl.
4. Add the salad dressing to the bean mixture and blend carefully. Taste for seasoning.
5. Line a salad bowl with the lettuce leaves and spoon the bean salad onto them. Garnish with the tomato wedges, sprinkled with the remaining basil.

Serves 4.

3

Soups

Soup is a perennial favorite in the United States. We dip into ten million bowls yearly, and nine out of ten American families serve soup at least once every three days.

Legumes lead as soup-makers; beans and split peas are the most popular. Ten ounces of a legume soup provide more vitamin A than two heads of lettuce, twelve ears of corn, four tomatoes, or nine eggs, and more protein and thiamine than rye bread.

You'll forget the health aspects, though, when you try the following soup recipes—they all taste so heartily good that you'll have to nudge yourself to remember that eating them is also good for you and provides almost as much protein as a serving of red meat.

Bean Soup—
A Variation

When we cook up a batch of baked beans we always save some for this soup, which has become a family favorite.

2 cups leftover baked beans
2 large onions, peeled and finely chopped
1 quart water
One 14½-ounce can tomatoes, drained and finely chopped
3 tablespoons butter or margarine
2 tablespoons flour
1 cup white wine (optional)
1 cup ditalini pasta, cooked al dente and drained
Salt to taste (optional)

1. Place beans in a pot large enough to hold all ingredients. Stir in the onions and water. Bring to a boil, then reduce heat and simmer 30 minutes, covered.
2. Stir in the tomatoes and simmer 20 minutes, covered.
3. In a saucepan, over medium heat, melt the butter or margarine. Stir in the flour, mixing and cooking into a smooth paste. Gradually add the wine, stirring into a smooth sauce.
4. Add the wine sauce to the bean pot. Stir in the cooked pasta. Taste for seasoning, adding salt, if needed.
5. Serve the bean soup very hot, with warm Italian bread for dipping.

Serves 6.

Charles Virion's
Country Bean Soup

Our friend, master chef Charles Virion, was a dedicated legume lover. This soup was a favorite of his.

3 tablespoons butter or margarine
4 medium-sized carrots, scraped and sliced
2 medium-sized turnips, scraped and diced
2 large onions, peeled and chopped
1 large leek, thoroughly cleaned and chopped, using all but the last inch of dark green
2 celery stalks, scraped and sliced
8 cups homemade Chicken Broth (page 13), or canned
One 16-ounce can cannellini beans (white kidney beans), drained, rinsed, and drained again
Salt and freshly ground black pepper to taste
8 thick slices from a large loaf of French bread, toasted
2 tablespoons chopped fresh chervil or parsley

1. In a deep pot, over medium heat, melt the butter or margarine. Add the carrots, turnips, onions, leek, and celery and cook, covered, stirring occasionally, for 8 minutes. Do not brown.
2. Pour in the chicken broth. Over low heat, cook, covered, for 35 minutes, or until the vegetables are tender.
3. Add the beans. Simmer, uncovered, for 5 minutes.
4. Taste for seasoning, adding salt and pepper to taste.
5. Spoon soup over the toasted bread in individual bowls. Lightly sprinkle with chervil or parsley.

Serves 8.

Western Black Bean Soup

A rich, classic soup that is a complete meal in itself. It has a delicate flavor but a hearty, satisfying texture.

  2 cups dried black beans
  1 meaty ham bone or a smoked ham hock (optional)
  2 medium-sized onions, peeled and chopped
  1 whole onion, stuck with 3 whole cloves
  2 celery stalks, scraped and chopped
  2 carrots, scraped and chopped
  ¼ teaspoon mace
  ¼ teaspoon dried thyme
  1½ quarts water
  1 quart homemade Chicken Broth (page 13), or canned
  Salt and freshly ground black pepper to taste
  ¼ cup dry sherry (optional)
  1 lemon, thinly sliced, seeds removed

1. Pick over the beans. Cover beans with 2 inches of water and bring to a boil. Boil 2 minutes, remove from heat, and soak, covered, for 1 hour. Drain.
2. Place the beans in a large soup pot. Add the ham bone or hock, chopped onions, onion with the cloves, celery, carrots, mace, thyme, water, and chicken broth. Bring to a boil and simmer, partially covered (prop the cover with a wooden spoon laid across the top of the pot), for 1½ hours, or until the beans can easily be mashed against the side of the pot with a spoon.
3. Remove the ham bone or hock, cutting the meat into small pieces. Reserve the meat.
4. Remove and discard the onion with cloves.
5. Run the soup through a food mill, blender, or food processor to purée. If too thick, stir in some chicken broth to obtain desired consistency.

6. Return the soup to the pot. Taste for seasoning, adding salt and pepper as needed.
7. Just before serving, bring to a simmer, and stir in the cut-up meat and sherry. Float 1 or 2 lemon slices on the top of each serving.

Serves 6.

Shell-Back Soup

This rich, smooth soup uses so-called turtle beans, which really are the widely available black beans.

Two 16-ounce cans black or turtle beans
2 tablespoons extra virgin olive oil
5 slices lean thick-sliced bacon, diced (optional)
1 small sweet red pepper, cored, seeded, and diced
1 medium-sized red onion, peeled and diced
1 garlic clove, peeled and minced
One 10½-ounce can turtle chowder
½ cup dry red wine (optional)
1½ cups homemade Chicken Broth (page 13), or canned
Salt and freshly ground black pepper to taste
Very thin lemon slices, seeds removed

1. Drain beans, rinse in cold water, and drain again. Reserve.
2. In a large pot, over medium heat, heat the olive oil. Cook the bacon for 6 minutes, or until golden.
3. Add the red pepper, onion, and garlic and cook 10 minutes, or until the pepper and onion are soft but not brown.
4. Stir in the reserved black beans, the turtle chowder, wine, chicken broth, and salt and pepper. Simmer for 10 minutes, or until very hot, but do not boil. Taste for seasoning.
5. Serve in warm soup bowls, garnished with lemon slices.

Serves 4.

Tiny Pasta Shell Soup
with Beans

Italians discovered many years ago that beans and pasta are a perfect match, making an especially lusty soup. They like their cooked dried beans al dente, or just slightly chewy, so the soaking method here is a little different from that in some other recipes.

2 cups dried Great Northern beans
2 quarts water
1 tablespoon salt
2 celery stalks, scraped and chopped
2 small white onions, peeled and chopped
3 tablespoons extra virgin olive oil
6 large very ripe tomatoes, peeled, seeded, and diced, or 1
   large can Italian tomatoes, including juice
1 tablespoon chopped fresh Italian parsley
4 fresh basil leaves, chopped, or 1 teaspoon dried
5 cups homemade Chicken Broth (page 13), or canned
½ pound *conchigliette* (tiny pasta shells)

1. Pick over the beans, removing any foreign material. Soak the beans in water for 6 hours. Drain.
2. Place the beans in a large pot, and add the water and 1 teaspoon salt. Bring to a boil, reduce heat, and simmer, covered, for 1 hour, until the beans are somewhat firm but nearly done. Taste to make sure. If the beans are still too firm, continue cooking. Drain and set aside.
3. In a deep saucepan, over medium heat, sauté the celery and onions in the oil until soft. Do not brown. Sprinkle in 1 teaspoon salt. Stir in the tomatoes, parsley, basil, and broth. Simmer for 15 minutes, uncovered, breaking up the tomatoes with a wooden spoon as they cook. Add the beans, blending well.
4. Cook the tiny shells in boiling water with the remaining 1 teaspoon salt until al dente, or slightly chewy. Drain and stir the pasta into the hot bean mixture. Serve in hot soup bowls.

Serves 4 to 6.

Curried Fresh Green
Pea Soup

2 tablespoons extra virgin olive oil
9 medium-sized shallots, peeled and finely chopped
1 tablespoon mild curry powder
⅛ teaspoon ground cumin
3 pounds freshly picked green peas, shelled
4 cups homemade Chicken Broth (page 13), or canned
Thinly peeled rind (in one strip) from 1 small lemon
Salt and freshly ground black pepper to taste
1 cup plain low-fat yogurt
2 tablespoons chopped fresh broad-leaf parsley for
   garnish

1. Heat the olive oil in a pot large enough to accommodate all ingredients. Add the shallots and cook for 5 minutes.
2. Stir in the curry powder and cumin. Add the peas, chicken broth, lemon rind, and salt and pepper.
3. Bring to a boil, reduce heat to low, and simmer for 15 minutes, or until the peas are just tender.
4. Discard lemon rind and push pea mixture through a food mill into a large bowl.
5. Cool pea purée and blend in the yogurt. Serve in soup bowls at room temperature, or chill as a summer soup. Garnish with fresh parsley.

Serves 6.

Quick Green Pea and Shrimp Soup

Here's a soup that's easy to make but has an unusually savory, piquant taste. Add a garnish of chopped chives for a pretty touch.

> 12 medium-sized shrimp, shelled and deveined
> Two 10-ounce cans green pea soup
> One 14-ounce can clear chicken broth
> 2 ounces dry sherry (optional)
> Salt to taste
> ½ cup half-and-half
> 2 tablespoons chopped chives for garnish

1. Simmer shrimp in boiling water just until pink; drain, then cut into very thin slices, almost shredded. Reserve.
2. In a large pot, blend the pea soup and chicken broth, stirring and simmering over medium heat.
3. Stir in the shrimp, sherry, and salt. When the soup is very hot, add the half-and-half, blending well.
4. Ladle soup into warm soup bowls and garnish with chopped chives.

Serves 4.

Lentils and Escarole Soup

This is a favorite family dish created by our mother and mother-in-law, Maria Limoncelli. She proved that lentils can combine with bland greens to make an original, outstanding soup.

1½ cups dried lentils
1 large head escarole, trimmed
8 cups homemade Chicken Broth (page 13), or canned
2 eggs
⅓ cup freshly grated Asiago or Parmesan cheese
Salt and freshly ground black pepper to taste

1. Pick over the lentils, discarding any foreign material. Rinse well and drain. Place lentils in a pot, cover with water, cover pot, and bring to a boil over high heat. Reduce heat to low and simmer for 20 minutes, or until the lentils are tender but not mushy. Drain and reserve.
2. Cut out the core from the head of escarole and discard. Rinse the leaves in 4 changes of fresh cold water, and drain.
3. Place the escarole in a pot and cover with water. Cover pot, bring to a boil over high heat, then reduce heat to low and simmer for 15 minutes, or until tender.
4. Drain the escarole well, then cool. With your hands, press the leaves to extract excess moisture. Chop the escarole. Reserve.
5. Pour the chicken broth into the now-empty escarole pot. Add the chopped escarole. In a bowl, beat the eggs. Add the cheese, beating and blending well with the eggs.
6. Over high heat, bring the chicken broth (and escarole) to a boil. Reduce heat to low and, with the stock at a simmer, slowly add the egg-cheese mixture, stirring well as it enters the pot.
7. Stir in the reserved lentils. Taste for seasoning, adding salt and pepper as needed. Simmer for 10 minutes. Serve hot with warm crusty bread.

Serves 6.

Lentils with Potato Soup

Lentils dramatically improve the flavor of this perennial favorite. This is a rather thick soup, as that is the way we like it.

> 1½ cups dried lentils
> 2 tablespoons extra virgin olive oil
> 4 large shallots, peeled and chopped
> 2 celery stalks, scraped and chopped
> 5 large Idaho potatoes, peeled and thinly sliced
> 6 cups beef stock, homemade or canned
> Salt and freshly ground black pepper to taste

1. Pick over lentils, discarding any foreign material. Rinse well and drain. Place in a pot and cover with water by 1 inch. Bring to a boil over high heat, reduce heat to low, and simmer for 20 minutes, or until lentils are tender but not too soft or mushy. Drain and reserve.
2. In a deep saucepan, over medium heat, heat the olive oil and sauté the shallots for 5 minutes, or until soft. Do not brown. Add the celery and cook for 5 minutes.
3. Add the potatoes and beef stock to the shallot pan. Season with salt and pepper. Bring to a boil, reduce heat to low, cover pan, and cook potatoes 20 minutes, or until they begin to break up. Stir occasionally while cooking.
4. Whisk the potatoes over low heat until they resemble a coarse purée. Blend in the drained, reserved lentils, stirring, until the lentil-potato soup is very hot. Taste for seasoning. Serve in warmed soup bowls, with warm rolls or crusty bread.

Serves 6.

Thick Lentil Soup

We first had this superb soup in an Armenian restaurant in Istanbul. We were so enthusiastic about it that the chef readily parted with the recipe. The garlicky yogurt is spread over the lentils.

 2 tablespoons olive oil
 1 large onion, peeled and chopped
 2 cups lentils, picked over, rinsed, and drained
 Four 15-ounce cans beef broth, or an equal amount of
     homemade
 Salt to taste
 1 pint plain low-fat yogurt
 1 garlic clove, peeled and minced

1. In a large pot, over medium heat, heat the oil and sauté the onion just until soft. Do not brown.
2. Stir in the lentils, and pour in the beef broth. Add the salt, but sparingly, as the broth may have provided enough. Cover the pot and simmer over low heat for 1 hour, or until lentils are very tender but not mushy. Taste for seasoning.
3. In a small bowl, blend the yogurt and garlic, and pass it at the table. Serve soup in warmed soup bowls, along with crusty Italian bread.

Serves 4.

Lentils with Little Tubes

We discovered this hearty *lenticchie* (lentil) soup in the regal old Albergo Excelsior in Florence, not too far from the Ponte Vecchio. The restaurant used a zesty prosciutto bone in this dish, but a ham bone will do just as well.

    ½ pound dried lentils
    3 quarts water
    1 leftover meaty ham bone
    2 teaspoons salt
    Freshly ground black pepper to taste
    3 tablespoons extra virgin olive oil
    2 medium-sized white onions, peeled and chopped
    2 large celery stalks with leaves, scraped and chopped
    ⅓ cup *tubetti* (small pasta tubes)
    ¼ cup freshly grated Parmesan cheese

1. Pick over lentils and rinse. Place in a large pot with the water, ham bone, 1 teaspoon salt, and the pepper. Simmer, covered, over medium heat, for 1 hour.
2. In a saucepan, over medium heat, heat 2 tablespoons olive oil and cook the onions and celery until soft, about 5 minutes. Do not brown. Stir the vegetables into the lentil pot. Simmer for 20 minutes, uncovered, stirring occasionally.
3. Cook the *tubetti* in boiling water, adding the remaining 1 teaspoon salt. Cook until al dente (just slightly chewy). Drain and stir into the lentil pot. Blend in the remaining 1 tablespoon olive oil and mill in more black pepper. Taste for seasoning.
4. Remove meat from the ham bone and dice. Discard bone. Stir meat into the lentil pot. Serve in individual soup bowls, sprinkled with the grated cheese.

Serves 4.

German Lentil Soup

At some German homes and restaurants you will find that 1 or 2 knockwurst (large frankfurters), skinned and cut into ¼-inch slices, are added to this soup for an even heartier texture and flavor.

If preferred, you can purée the soup in a blender or food processor (do not overprocess). In that case, instead of dicing the bacon, cut it into large pieces that can be easily removed, along with the ham bone and bay leaf, before puréeing. After puréeing, add the half-and-half and heat just to a simmer.

1 cup dried lentils
2 tablespoons butter or margarine
3 slices lean thick-cut bacon, diced
1 medium-sized onion, peeled and thinly sliced
1 medium-sized carrot, scraped and thinly sliced
1 celery stalk, scraped and thinly sliced
1 meaty ham bone or smoked ham hock
6 cups beef broth, canned or homemade
2 medium-sized potatoes, cut into ½-inch cubes
1 bay leaf
⅛ teaspoon dried marjoram
Salt and freshly ground black pepper to taste
1 cup half-and-half

1. Pick over the lentils and rinse them in several changes of water.
2. Over medium heat, melt the butter or margarine in a pot large enough to hold all ingredients. Add the bacon and onion and cook until the onion is soft. Do not brown. Add the carrot, celery, ham bone, lentils, and beef broth. Cover the pot and simmer over low heat for 1 hour, stirring occasionally, until the lentils are almost tender.
3. Add the potatoes, bay leaf, and marjoram. Simmer for 30 minutes, or until the potatoes and lentils are tender. Season with salt and pepper.

4. Cut any meat on the ham bone into small cubes. Discard bone. Add meat pieces to soup and simmer, uncovered, for 10 minutes.
5. Stir in the half-and-half and heat just to a simmer. Remove bay leaf and serve.

Serves 6.

Baby Lima Bean and
Lettuce Soup

You'll find that chopped watercress adds a peppery bite to this unusual soup. Croutons make an excellent finishing touch.

½ cup chopped watercress or parsley
1 small head romaine lettuce, cut into small pieces
4 cups homemade Chicken Broth (page 13), or canned
Two 10-ounce packages frozen baby limas, cooked
  according to package directions and well drained
Salt and freshly ground black pepper to taste
Croutons for garnish

1. Combine the watercress, lettuce, 2 cups chicken broth, and the limas in a blender or food processor. Whirl on high speed for 20 seconds, or until puréed but not soupy.
2. Place purée in a saucepan, adding the remaining chicken broth, and season lightly with salt and pepper. Blend well with a spoon, and simmer, stirring, over medium heat until very hot.
3. Serve in warm soup bowls with a generous sprinkling of croutons.

Serves 4.

Minestrone

This international favorite owes much of its popularity to its wealth of legumes. For a quicker version, use 1 cup each of canned chick-peas and kidney beans—drain and rinse them, then drain again. Add them last to the pot, just long enough to heat through.

½ cup dried chick-peas
½ cup dried white kidney beans
3 tablespoons olive oil
1 medium-sized onion, peeled and chopped
1 garlic clove, peeled and minced
1 cup chopped cabbage (do not use the core)
3 celery stalks, scraped and coarsely chopped
1 carrot, scraped and coarsely chopped
½ pound green string beans, trimmed and cut into ½-inch pieces
1 medium-sized potato, diced
One 1-pound can tomatoes (including liquid), coarsely chopped
2 quarts homemade Chicken Broth (page 13), or canned
½ cup of *ditalini* (short tubular pasta) or any other small soup pasta
Salt and freshly ground black pepper to taste
⅛ teaspoon dried red pepper flakes (optional)
½ cup freshly grated Asiago or Parmesan cheese

1. Pick over chick-peas and kidney beans. Put in large pot and cover with 2 inches of water. Bring to a boil and boil 2 minutes. Remove from heat and soak, covered, 1 hour. Drain.
2. Put the chick-peas and beans in 2 quarts of salted water, bring to a boil, reduce heat, and simmer for 1 hour, or until just tender (do not overcook, as they cook more later), and drain.
3. In a large pot, over medium heat, heat the olive oil and sauté the onion and garlic until soft. Do not brown. Add the cabbage,

celery, carrot, string beans, and potato and cook for 2 minutes, stirring.

4. Add the tomatoes and broth and simmer, stirring occasionally, 30 minutes, or until the vegetables are tender.

5. Stir in the cooked chick-peas, beans, and pasta. Cook for 10 minutes, or until the pasta is al dente (slightly chewy).

6. Season with salt and pepper. Stir in the red pepper flakes, if desired.

7. Serve hot with a spoonful of grated cheese sprinkled over each serving.

Serves 6 to 8.

Pistou

1 pound pea beans, picked over
2 quarts water
1 quart beef stock, homemade or canned
4 medium-sized leeks, white part only, thoroughly cleaned and finely diced
3 large, ripe tomatoes, peeled, seeded, and chopped, or one 14-ounce can plum tomatoes, with liquid
3 small fresh sage leaves, or 1 teaspoon dried
1½ teaspoons salt, or to taste
½ teaspoon freshly ground pepper
1 pound fresh yellow string beans, cut into ½-inch pieces
3 new potatoes, peeled, cut into ½-inch cubes
4 small zucchini, cut into cubes slightly larger than the potatoes
2 cups canned chick-peas, drained, rinsed, and drained again
4 ounces vermicelli pasta, broken up
Pistou Mixture (recipe follows)

1. Cover beans with 2 inches of water, boil 2 minutes, remove from heat, and soak, covered, for 1 hour. Drain.
2. In a large pot, bring the drained beans, 2 quarts water, and beef stock to a boil. Reduce heat to low and simmer, partially covered, for 40 minutes.
3. Add the leeks, tomatoes, sage, salt, and pepper. Simmer for 30 minutes, stirring frequently, until the beans are almost tender.
4. Add the string beans, potatoes, and zucchini and simmer, uncovered, 15 minutes, stirring occasionally, until the vegetables are just tender.
5. Stir in the chick-peas and vermicelli and cook 5 minutes, or until the pasta is cooked al dente—slightly chewy.
6. Just before serving, stir in the pistou, blending it well with the vegetables and pasta. Taste for seasoning.

Serves 6 to 8.

Pistou Mixture

½ cup extra virgin olive oil
¾ cup grated Romano cheese
5 garlic cloves, peeled
6 large fresh basil leaves

Place all ingredients in a blender or food processor and blend into a smooth paste.

Red Bean Soup à la Scott

An easy and delicious soup for a quick supper, especially when accompanied by thick slices of warm Italian bread. Easy because the beans come from a can and the tomato sauce from the freezer; delicious, because the beans and sauce combine beautifully. Freeze the sauce in 1-cup portions.

  Two 16-ounce cans cannellini beans (white kidney beans), drained, rinsed, and drained again
  3 cups homemade Chicken Broth (page 13), or canned
  1 teaspoon freshly ground black pepper
  1 cup Filetto di Pomodoro Sauce (recipe follows)
  ¼ cup freshly grated Asiago or Parmesan cheese
  Salt to taste

1. Combine the beans and broth in a pot, heat, and simmer, stirring carefully, for 2 minutes.
2. With the heat low, add the pepper. Stir in the *filetto* sauce and 1 tablespoon cheese.
3. Cook, stirring, for 3 minutes. Taste for seasoning, adding salt, if necessary. (The broth may have supplied enough.)
4. Serve in hot soup bowls with remaining cheese sprinkled over each serving.

Serves 4 to 6.

Filetto di Pomodoro Sauce

  3 tablespoons extra virgin olive oil
  3 large onions, peeled and chopped
  1 tablespoon dried sweet basil
  Two 2-pound, 3-ounce cans Italian plum tomatoes, put through a food mill

1 teaspoon salt
½ teaspoon freshly ground black pepper

1. Heat the olive oil in a saucepan and sauté the onions for 3 minutes, over medium heat. Do not brown. Reduce heat and stir in the basil. Cook, stirring, for 3 minutes.
2. Stir in the tomatoes; cook, stirring frequently, for 20 minutes.
3. Add the salt and pepper, blending well into the tomatoes. Raise heat, stir, and cook off any excess liquid from the tomato sauce. Taste for seasoning. The sauce is ready when you can pull a wooden spoon lightly through the sauce without leaving a watery trail.

Makes approximately 7 cups.

Puŕee of Light Red
Kidney Bean Soup

We like to offer this unusual soup as a first course. You can save the pork butt for another meal. Slice it hot or cold, and combine with another legume—perhaps a side dish of hot lentils.

2 tablespoons butter or margarine
1 large onion, peeled and finely chopped
3 celery stalks, scraped and minced
3 small carrots, scraped and minced
6 sprigs parsley, 2 whole cloves, and 3 whole allspice tied together in a cheesecloth bag
One 2-pound smoked, cured pork butt
3 cups beef broth, homemade or canned
3 cups water
Two 15-ounce cans light red kidney beans, drained, rinsed, and drained again
Salt and freshly ground black pepper to taste
¾ cup dry sherry (optional)
¼ teaspoon cayenne
4 hard-boiled eggs, coarsely chopped, for garnish
1 large lemon, thinly sliced, for garnish

1. Heat the butter or margarine in a large, deep pot and sauté the onion for 5 minutes, stirring. Do not brown.
2. Stir in the celery, carrots, and bag containing parsley, cloves, and allspice. Add the pork butt.
3. Cover with the beef broth and water. Bring to a boil over high heat. Cover, reduce heat to low, and simmer for 1½ hours, or until pork is tender.
4. Remove the pork and save it for another meal. Remove and discard the bag of parsley and spices. Skim off any fat.
5. Stir the beans into the pot. Simmer, covered, for 15 minutes.
6. Using a blender or food processor, purée the soup.

7. Return the soup to the pot and simmer, stirring, over low heat, seasoning with salt and pepper. Stir in the sherry, if desired, and cayenne and cook for 5 minutes.
8. Serve the bean soup in warm bowls, each portion garnished with chopped egg and a slice of lemon.

Serves 8.

Split Pea Soup with Chicken Frankfurters

Chicken or turkey franks are lower in fat and calories than meat franks, and they taste just as good. Coupled with split peas in this recipe, they help to make a good soup even better.

1½ cups dried split peas
1 large red onion, peeled and chopped
1 teaspoon salt
½ teaspoon freshly ground black pepper
2 tablespoons butter or margarine
½ pound chicken franks, chopped

1. Pick over split peas, discarding any foreign material. Rinse well and drain.
2. Place the peas in a pot, cover with water, and stir in the onion, salt, and pepper. Cover pot, bring to a boil over high heat, then reduce heat to low. Simmer for 20 minutes, or until the split peas are tender, but not soft or mushy.
3. Over medium heat, melt butter or margarine in a frying pan and cook the chopped franks, stirring, for 5 minutes, or until lightly browned.
4. Stir the franks and butter into the soup pot, and simmer for 5 minutes, blending flavors. Taste for seasoning.

Serves 4.

Dutch Split Pea Soup

A ham bone isn't essential for a good split pea soup, but it does give this soup its style and authenticity.

2 cups green split peas, picked over and washed in several changes of water
½ cup diced salt pork, or 2 tablespoons vegetable oil
1 large leek, thoroughly cleaned and chopped (use all the white part and the light green part)
1 medium-sized onion, peeled and chopped
1 celery stalk, scraped and coarsely chopped
1 medium-sized carrot, scraped and coarsely chopped
1 garlic clove, mashed; ⅛ teaspoon dried thyme; 1 bay leaf; and 2 springs parsley tied in a piece of cheesecloth
8 cups homemade Chicken Broth (page 13), or canned
1 meaty ham bone, if available
Salt and freshly ground black pepper to taste
2 tablespoons butter or margarine (optional)
½ cup heavy cream or half-and-half

1. In a large pot, cover the peas with water and bring to a boil. Remove from the heat and let stand 1 hour, covered.
2. Meanwhile, cook the salt pork in a frying pan until golden brown. Remove pork with a slotted spoon and discard, leaving the fat in the pan. (Or use 2 tablespoons vegetable oil in place of salt pork.)
3. Add the leek, onion, celery, and carrot to the fat or oil in the pan and sauté over low heat until they are soft. Do not brown.
4. Drain the peas, and return them to their pot. Remove vegetables from the pan with a slotted spoon and add to peas, along with the cheesecloth bag, broth, and ham bone.
5. Bring to a boil, reduce heat, and simmer 30 minutes to 1 hour, or until the peas can be mashed against the side of the pot. Stir occasionally to prevent scorching.

6. Remove and discard the cheesecloth bag. Remove the ham bone, cut the meat from it into small pieces and reserve. Discard bone.
7. Push the soup through a sieve or food mill or blend coarsely in a blender. Return to the pot. Taste and season with salt and pepper.
8. Just before serving, add the butter or margarine, if desired, and the cream or half-and-half, and stir.
9. Serve very hot, garnished with the bits of ham.

Serves 4 to 6.

White Bean, Italian Sausage, Potato, Red Pepper Soup

3 tablespoons unsalted butter or margarine
6 scallions, white part only, diced
3 stalks celery, scraped and diced
1 large sweet red pepper, seeded, cored, and diced
Two 1-pound cans cannellini beans, drained and rinsed
1 large Idaho potato, boiled in water until tender, and diced
2 sweet and 2 hot Italian sausages, broiled, drained, skinned, and diced
6 cups homemade Chicken Broth (page 13), or canned
Salt and freshly ground black pepper to taste
3 tablespoons minced fresh broad-leaf parsley for garnish

1. Melt the butter or margarine in a saucepan large enough to hold all ingredients. In it, sauté the scallions, celery, and red pepper until soft. Do not brown.
2. Add the beans, diced potato, sausages, and chicken broth, stirring well to blend. Taste and season with salt and pepper (the chicken broth may supply enough salt). Stir.
3. Serve in large rimmed soup bowls; garnish each serving with minced parsley.

Serves 6 to 8.

4

Salads

Come hot summer days, many of us serve salads as the main meal. Legumes, with all their diversity, can make the difference between an interesting or run-of-the-mill offering.

What about a chick-pea salad with cooled, shredded cod? Or a baby lima bean salad with lobster, or the classic niçoise salad? We suggest serving our salad made with three different types of beans, or you can pair a legume salad with soup or sandwiches for a quick, satisfying meal.

Never before have salads had it so good—or been so appealing. Thanks to legumes, of course.

Baby Lima Bean Salad

We first had this delicious salad in Frankfurt accompanied by broiled veal sausages as only the Germans can make them.

- 2 cups dried baby lima beans
- 1 small red onion, peeled, thinly sliced, then coarsely chopped
- 1 cup sour cream or plain low-fat yogurt
- ½ cup chopped fresh chives
- 2 tablespoons balsamic vinegar
- 1 teaspoon prepared horseradish
- 1 teaspoon salt
- ½ teaspoon freshly ground black pepper
- ¼ cup chopped watercress for garnish

1. Soak beans overnight or use quick-soaking method: Cover with water and boil for 2 minutes, cover, and soak 1 to 2 hours. Drain. Cover with fresh water and cook, covered, at a simmer, for 1 hour, or until beans are tender. Do not overcook beans or they will shed their skins and become too soft. Drain well.
2. Combine the beans and onion in a bowl, tossing carefully but well.
3. In another bowl, combine the sour cream or yogurt, chives, vinegar, horseradish, salt, and pepper, blending well. Taste for seasoning.
4. Mix this salad dressing with the beans and onion. Serve sprinkled with the chopped watercress.

Serves 4.

Baby Lima Bean Salad with Lobster and Potato

Other cooked beans can be substituted for the limas in this impressive entrée salad. In a pinch, you can use canned or frozen lima beans.

2 cups fresh baby lima beans
3 medium-sized new potatoes
Boston lettuce leaves
Two 1½-pound cooked lobsters, meat removed and cubed; reserve the upper half of the shells and keep the claws intact
1 tablespoon chopped canned red pimiento
1½ cups mayonnaise mixed with 3 tablespoons freshly squeezed lemon juice
Salt to taste

1. Simmer the lima beans in lightly salted water for 2 minutes, cover, and soak for 1 to 2 hours. Drain. Cover again with water and cook, covered, at a simmer for 1 hour until tender but still slightly firm. Do not overcook. Drain and set aside.
2. Boil the potatoes in their skins until tender, drain, and dry over heat in the pan. Cool. Peel, cube, and set aside.
3. Line a salad bowl with lettuce leaves.
4. In another bowl, combine the potatoes, three-quarters of the lobster meat, the pimiento, and half the mayonnaise mixture. Toss well but carefully. Taste and add salt and more mayonnaise, if needed.
5. Mound the lobster salad on the lettuce in the bowl. Sprinkle the lima beans prominently on and around the salad. Rim with the remaining lobster meat. Garnish with dabs of mayonnaise, and the lobster claws.
6. Upend, pyramid fashion, the upper halves of the lobster shells in the center of the salad, and serve.

Serves 4.

Cannellini Bean Salad

An easy but pleasing accompaniment to grilled meats, fish, or poultry.

Two 1-pound cans cannellini beans
¼ cup chopped fresh broad-leaf parsley, plus additional
    for garnish
1 celery stalk, scraped and finely diced
1 small garlic clove, peeled and minced
Approximately 2 tablespoons olive oil
1 tablespoon red wine vinegar, or to taste
Salt and freshly ground black pepper to taste
Romaine lettuce leaves

1. Drain the beans into a strainer and rinse under cold running water.
2. In a bowl, combine the beans, parsley, celery, and garlic. Pour on the olive oil and toss very gently, avoiding crushing the beans.
3. Add the vinegar and salt and pepper and toss gently again. Taste for seasoning, adding more oil, vinegar, and seasonings, if desired.
4. Line a salad bowl with the lettuce leaves, spoon in the salad, and sprinkle additional parsley over the beans.

Serves 4.

Chick-peas and Cod Salad

1   pound dried boneless salted cod
½   pound dried chick-peas
1   large onion, peeled and stuck with 1 clove
1   teaspoon salt
½   cup milk
½   teaspoon dried thyme
1   garlic clove, peeled and minced
1   medium-sized red onion, peeled and diced
2   large ripe tomatoes, peeled and chopped
2   tablespoons chopped watercress
⅓   cup extra virgin olive oil
¼   cup red wine vinegar
   Salt and freshly ground black pepper to taste

1. Soak cod in water 12 hours, changing water 4 times.
2. Pick over chick-peas, discarding any foreign material. Soak, covered with water, overnight; or boil in water 2 minutes, remove from heat, cover, and soak 1 to 2 hours. Drain, rinse, and drain again. Place in a soup pot, adding the cloved onion and salt. Cover beans with water, bring to a boil over high heat, reduce heat to medium, and simmer 2 hours, or until chick-peas are tender but not too soft or mushy. Discard onion and clove. Reserve chick-peas in pot, draining any liquid remaining.
3. Drain cod and place in a deep saucepan. Barely cover cod with water, adding milk and thyme. Bring to a boil over high heat, reduce heat to medium, and simmer for 15 minutes, or until fish flakes with a fork. Drain, cool, and shred cod.
4. Place reserved cooked chick-peas in a large salad bowl in one layer. Arrange the shredded cod over the chick-peas.
5. Add garlic, red onion, tomatoes, watercress, olive oil, and vinegar. Toss carefully with 2 forks to blend. Taste for seasoning, adding salt and pepper as needed.

Serves 4 to 6.

Chick-pea, Cucumber, and Radish Salad

One 16-ounce can chick-peas, drained, rinsed, and drained
    again
1 medium-sized cucumber, peeled, cut into quarters
    lengthwise, seeded, and cut into small bite-sized pieces
1 cup sliced small radishes
½ green pepper, seeded, trimmed, and chopped
1 large celery stalk, scraped and chopped
Boston lettuce leaves

Salad Dressing

5 tablespoons olive oil
2 tablespoons red wine vinegar
Salt and freshly ground black pepper to taste

1. In a large bowl, combine and mix well the chick-peas, cucumber,
    radishes, green pepper, and celery.
2. Whisk together salad dressing ingredients in small bowl.
3. Pour the salad dressing into the chick-pea mixture and mix well.
    Taste for seasoning.
4. Serve on the lettuce leaves.

Serves 4.

Fava Bean Salad

Lemon Dressing

2   tablespoons freshly squeezed lemon juice
6   tablespoons extra virgin olive oil
1   teaspoon salt
½   teaspoon freshly ground black pepper

Two 16-ounce cans fava beans, drained, rinsed, and
    drained again
½   cup chopped bread-and-butter pickles
6   pitted black olives, chopped
6   green, pimiento-stuffed olives, chopped
½   cup celery, scraped and diced
2   tablespoons chopped scallions, white part only
Lettuce leaves

1. In a small bowl, blend lemon dressing ingredients, and set aside.
2. In a large bowl, combine the beans, pickles, olives, celery, and scallions.
3. Spoon on the lemon dressing and toss well but lightly with 2 forks. Refrigerate until ready to serve. Taste for seasoning.
4. Serve each portion on lettuce leaves on individual salad plates.

Serves 6.

German Green Bean Salad

Almond slivers, crisped in butter, add a special crunch to this salad.

Salad Dressing

½ cup extra virgin olive oil
3 tablespoons freshly squeezed lemon juice
Salt and freshly ground black pepper to taste

1 pound fresh tender green beans, cooked in unsalted
   boiling water 10 minutes, or until crisp-tender
1 medium-sized red Italian onion, peeled and thinly sliced
1 tablespoon chopped fresh parsley
4 fresh mint leaves, chopped
2 tablespoons browned almond slivers (optional)

1. In a small bowl, blend the oil, lemon juice, salt, and pepper.
2. While the beans are still warm, toss with half the dressing. Add
   the onion, parsley, and mint and blend.
3. Taste for seasoning, adding more dressing according to taste.
4. Chill before serving. Sprinkle each portion with sautéed almond
   slivers, if you like.

Serves 4.

Yellow Snap Bean Slaw

1½ pounds fresh yellow snap beans, cut into 1-inch pieces,
    cooked in salted boiling water until crisp-tender,
    drained
 1 cup shredded, young, tender cabbage leaves
 1 cup scraped, shredded carrot
 1 medium-sized red onion, peeled and finely chopped
 2 celery stalks, scraped and chopped
 ¼ teaspoon dried oregano
Salt and freshly ground black pepper to taste
 5 tablespoons mayonnaise
 2 tablespoons freshly squeezed lemon juice
 3 tablespoons chopped fresh parsley, plus additional for
    garnish
Lettuce leaves

1. Combine all ingredients, except lettuce leaves, in a bowl and mix
   well.
2. Add more mayonnaise, if needed. Taste for seasoning.
3. Spoon mixture onto lettuce leaves on individual salad plates.
   Sprinkle with additional parsley and serve.

Serves 4 to 6.

Grill-Master Beans

This bean salad is an excellent companion to grilled swordfish steaks. Or to grilled meats and chicken, for that matter.

Two 16-ounce cans red kidney beans, drained, rinsed, and drained again
4 hard-boiled eggs, coarsely chopped
4 large celery stalks, scraped and diced
2 medium-sized carrots, scraped and grated
½ cup pickle relish
½ cup chopped scallions, white part only
½ cup shredded sharp Cheddar cheese
Approximately 1 cup sour cream or plain low-fat yogurt
Boston lettuce leaves
Chopped fresh parsley for garnish

1. Combine the kidney beans, eggs, celery, carrots, pickle relish, scallions, and cheese in a large bowl and mix gently.
2. Gently stir in half the sour cream or yogurt, blending well. Taste for seasoning. Add more sour cream or yogurt, if desired. Chill.
3. Serve on the lettuce leaves and sprinkle with the parsley.

Serves 4 to 6.

Hassan's Bean Salad

During a stint as a war correspondent in Cairo many years ago, the male half of this team was often served this simple but pleasing salad by Hassan, a Sudanese cook.

Salad Dressing

2 teaspoons salt
2 whole garlic cloves, peeled
¼ cup virgin olive oil
⅓ cup strained freshly squeezed orange juice

1½ cups dried white pea beans
8 Bibb lettuce leaves
3 tablespoons finely chopped sweet Vidalia onions
3 tablespoons chopped broad-leaf parsley

1. Blend together all ingredients for salad dressing. Reserve.
2. Pick over the beans, discarding any foreign material and imperfect beans. Rinse well. Place in a pot, cover with water, and bring to a boil. Boil 2 minutes, remove from heat, cover, and let stand 1 to 2 hours. Drain.
3. Cover beans with water and bring to a boil over medium heat. Cover, reduce heat to low, and simmer for 25 minutes, or until the beans are just tender. Drain and cool beans.
4. Transfer beans to a bowl, pour in the dressing mixture, and toss well. Chill 3 hours. Remove and discard the garlic. Spoon the mixture over lettuce leaves on individual plates. Mix the onions and parsley and sprinkle on the salads before serving.

Serves 4.

Fresh Three-Legume Salad

Fresh legumes from the garden are not always readily available, so in this recipe you can use the dried, canned, or frozen variety. But try for fresh ones. Their exceptional taste is worth the effort.

Salad Dressing

⅓ cup balsamic vinegar
½ cup light olive oil
⅓ teaspoon dry mustard
1 teaspoon salt
1 teaspoon sugar
4 anchovies, rinsed, dried, and chopped
2 tablespoons small capers, rinsed and dried

2 pounds fresh small green peas, shelled
½ pound fresh shell beans (any of the white beans, or baby limas), shelled
½ pound fresh small yellow string or snap (green) beans, trimmed
1 small turnip, scraped and cut in strips
5 small carrots, scraped and cut in strips
Salt

1. Combine dressing ingredients in a screw-top jar and shake well. Reserve.
2. Cook the vegetables separately in boiling, salted water until tender but still crisp. Do not overcook—3 to 10 minutes should be enough time.
3. Drain the vegetables, rinse in cold water, drain again, and pat dry on paper towels. Combine them in a large bowl.
4. Pour on half the salad dressing and blend well. Taste for seasoning. Add more salad dressing, if necessary. Refrigerate to marinate for 1½ hours.
5. Serve the salad over lettuce leaves on individual plates, or spoon beside individual servings of fish, fowl, or meat of your choice.

Serves 4.

Lentil-Scallion Salad

1 cup dried lentils
2 cups homemade Chicken Broth (page 13), or canned
Salt and freshly ground black pepper to taste
⅓ cup extra virgin olive oil
2 tablespoons balsamic vinegar
4 scallions, white part only, finely chopped
½ cup chopped parsley

1. Pick over lentils and rinse well. Place in a pot with the chicken broth, cover, and bring to a boil. Lower heat and simmer 30 minutes, or until tender. Drain.
2. Add salt, pepper, oil, and vinegar to lentils. Cool to room temperature.
3. Add scallions and half the chopped parsley. Blend. Taste for seasoning.
4. Garnish with remaining parsley.

Serves 4.

Niçoise Legume Salad

Salad Dressing

¼ cup vinegar, preferably balsamic
¾ cup extra virgin olive oil
Salt and freshly ground black pepper to taste
½ teaspoon sugar
½ teaspoon Dijon mustard

1 large head Bibb or Boston lettuce, washed, dried, and
  chilled
One 16-ounce can cannellini beans, drained, rinsed, and
  drained again
1 cup cooked lentils
1 cup cooked fresh green peas
½ pound fresh, tender string beans, simmered until crisp-
  tender, cooled, and cut into bite-sized pieces
1 medium-sized potato, boiled in its skin until tender,
  cooled, peeled, and cut into bite-sized cubes
One 7-ounce can solid albacore tuna, drained and broken
  into small chunks
3 ripe firm tomatoes, peeled, each cut into 6 wedges
2 teaspoons capers, rinsed and drained
½ cup pitted black olives, preferably Greek
2 hard-boiled eggs, quartered
6 anchovy fillets, drained
1 tablespoon chopped fresh tarragon or parsley for
  garnish

1. Combine and blend all dressing ingredients. Set aside.
2. Line a salad bowl with lettuce leaves.
3. In a large bowl, combine the cannellini beans, the lentils, green
   peas, string beans, potato, tuna, the wedges of 2 of the tomatoes, and the capers. Stir the salad dressing and add half to the
   mixture. Gently mix. Taste and add more salad dressing, if
   necessary.

4. Spoon mixture into a lettuce-lined salad bowl.
5. Garnish with the remaining tomato wedges, black olives, egg quarters, and anchovies. Sprinkle with chopped tarragon or parsley.

Serves 4 to 6.

Pinto Beans Abdullah

We discovered this unique cold bean salad at Abdullah's in Istanbul. It is traditionally served with sliced tomatoes.

> 1 pound dried pinto beans
> Salt to taste
> 1 cup Abdullah Sauce (recipe follows)
> 2 tablespoons chopped broad-leaf parsley for garnish

1. Pick over the beans, discarding any imperfect beans. Soak overnight or boil in water 2 minutes, remove from heat, cover, and soak 1 to 2 hours.
2. Drain the beans. Place in a pot, cover with salted water, and bring to a boil. Lower heat and simmer, covered, for 45 minutes, or until the beans are tender, but intact.
3. Drain the beans, and spoon into a serving bowl. Spoon the sauce over the beans.
4. Sprinkle with the parsley.

Serves 4.

Abdullah Sauce

1 cup walnuts
1 cup extra virgin olive oil
4 slices white bread, crusts removed, soaked in milk and squeezed dry
1 garlic clove, peeled and halved
1 teaspoon salt
⅛ cup white vinegar

1. Place half the nuts, half the oil, half the bread, half the garlic, and all of the salt in a blender container. Cover and turn the blender on high for several seconds.

2. Add the remaining ingredients and the vinegar. Cover and turn blender on low for a few seconds. The sauce should be smooth, but not too thick.
3. Refrigerate until ready to use.

Makes about 2 cups.

Light Red Kidney Bean Salad

Two 15-ounce cans light red kidney beans, undrained
1   cup chopped scallions, white part only
1   teaspoon salt
1   teaspoon brown sugar
¾   cup red wine vinegar
3   tablespoons freshly chopped watercress for garnish

1. Pour the beans with their liquid into a large bowl.
2. Blend in the scallions, salt, brown sugar, and red wine vinegar.
3. Cover and refrigerate overnight.
4. Before serving, drain off the liquid. Serve at room temperature with the chopped watercress sprinkled over the beans.

Serves 4.

Summer Garden Salad

1   cup dried black-eyed peas
1   pound string beans, cut up
1   pound small new potatoes
Vinaigrette Sauce (recipe follows)
2   ripe tomatoes, peeled and each cut into 3 wedges
1   medium-sized red onion, peeled, sliced and separated
    into rings
2   tablespoons chopped fresh basil

1. Pick over the dried peas. Cover with water and boil 2 minutes.
   Remove from heat, cover, and let stand 1 hour. Drain. Cover
   with water again and cook over medium heat for 1 hour, or until
   tender but not mushy. Drain well.
2. Cook the string beans in lightly salted boiling water, until ten-
   der-crisp. Drain.
3. Cook potatoes in lightly salted, boiling water until tender. Drain
   and slice (you can peel them or leave the skins on).
4. In a large salad bowl, toss well, but carefully, the cooked peas,
   beans, and potatoes with two-thirds of the sauce. Taste for seasoning, adding more sauce as desired.
5. Garnish with the tomato wedges and onion rings and sprinkle
   with basil.

Serves 6.

Vinaigrette Sauce

This is best served right after mixing, but it can be mixed well in
advance and whisked just before adding to the salad.

½   teaspoon Dijon mustard
1   teaspoon sugar
3   tablespoons red wine vinegar

Salt and freshly ground black pepper to taste
½ cup extra virgin olive oil

1. In a small bowl, whisk the mustard, sugar, vinegar, salt, and pepper.
2. Gradually whisk in the olive oil.

Makes slightly less than ¾ cup.

Three-Bean Salad

We find this dish makes a refreshing summer luncheon when served with chicken or tuna sandwiches. If cranberry beans aren't available, substitute the ever-reliable cannellini beans.

One 15-ounce can cranberry beans
One 15-ounce can pink beans
One 15-ounce can red kidney beans
1 large sweet red onion, peeled and finely chopped
2 tablespoons chopped parsley, plus additional for garnish
About ¾ cup Vinaigrette Sauce (page 83)
Boston lettuce leaves

1. Drain the canned beans, rinse well, and drain well again.
2. In a large bowl, combine the beans, onion, and parsley. Add half the sauce, blending well. Taste and add more sauce according to preference.
3. Serve the bean salad on individual plates lined with Boston lettuce leaves. Sprinkle a little parsley on each.

Serves 4 to 6.

5

Vegetable Dishes

When vegetable courses start to bore, try some of these imaginative and different legumes dishes in their place. Serve Antoine Gilly's Lentils in Red Wine, or our Black Bean Casserole. Peas and Cheese Balls are really unique, and Green Beans with Mushrooms will always please.

These dishes are fun to make, keep well, and are good for you.

Black Bean Casserole

We enjoyed this savory dish at a friend's table in Ireland. We like it just as it is for lunch, but serve it to guests for dinner with a chicken or fish dish. In Ireland, of course, we had salmon.

2 cups dried black beans
2 medium-sized onions, peeled and thinly sliced
2 large carrots, scraped and sliced
1 large celery stalk, scraped and sliced
2 small garlic cloves, peeled and left whole
Homemade Chicken Broth (page 13), or canned, to cover
    beans and vegetables
3 tablespoons finely chopped lean bacon
Salt and freshly ground black pepper to taste
⅛ teaspoon dried red pepper flakes, or according to taste
¼ cup Irish whiskey (optional)
Plain low-fat yogurt

1. Pick over beans, discarding any foreign material, and rinse. Soak beans overnight, or boil 2 minutes in 4 cups of water and let soak 1 to 2 hours.
2. Drain the beans, and put them in a pot with the onions, carrots, celery, and garlic. Cover with chicken broth. Cover and simmer over low heat for 1 hour. Remove and discard the garlic.
3. In a small frying pan over medium heat, cook the bacon until crisp and golden. Stir the bacon and its fat into the bean pot, along with a sprinkling of salt and black pepper. Blend in the red pepper flakes and the Irish whiskey, if desired.
4. Spoon this bean mixture into a casserole. Cook, covered, in a preheated 300 F oven for 1 hour, or until beans are tender.
5. Serve in the casserole, with an offering of yogurt on the side.

Serves 4 to 6.

Black Mung Beans Piccante

These slightly sweet soft beans add a piquant touch to a dinner of broiled swordfish or halibut.

     2 cups dried black mung beans
     3 cups homemade Chicken Broth (page 13), or canned
     3 tablespoons extra virgin olive oil
     8 scallions, white portion only, finely chopped
     2 garlic cloves, peeled and minced
     2 tablespoons capers, drained, dried, and chopped
        Freshly squeezed, strained juice of 2 lemons; save peel
     2 tablespoons chopped watercress or broad-leaf parsley

1. Soak beans in water for 1 hour. Drain.
2. Place beans in a pot and cover with chicken broth. Cover and cook over medium heat for 40 minutes, or until tender. If there is liquid left in the pot, drain the beans.
3. In a deep saucepan over low heat, heat the olive oil and sauté the scallions and garlic for 5 minutes, or until soft. Do not brown.
4. Add the beans, capers, and lemon juice and peel, blending well. Cover pan and simmer mixture, stirring occasionally, for 5 minutes.
5. Remove and discard the lemon peel. Stir in the watercress. Serve hot.

Serves 4.

Cuban Black Beans

1 pound dried black beans
1 green pepper, halved, seeded, and cored
1 medium-sized onion, peeled and stuck with 2 cloves
1 bay leaf
¼ teaspoon dried oregano
5 tablespoons extra virgin olive oil
1 green pepper, seeded, cored, and chopped
1 medium-sized onion, peeled and chopped
1 garlic clove, peeled and minced
½ teaspoon sugar dissolved in ¼ cup red wine vinegar
Salt to taste

1. Pick over the beans and rinse. Soak in cold water to cover 5 hours (or use the quicker method, see page 10).
2. Drain the beans and place them in a pot with the halved green pepper, the onion with the cloves, bay leaf, oregano, and 2 tablespoons olive oil. Barely cover the beans with cold water. Bring to a boil, reduce heat, and simmer, uncovered, for 1 hour, stirring occasionally, or until the beans are soft and there is very little liquid left in the pot. (Do not salt the beans while they are cooking. If the liquid cooks off before the beans are soft, add small amounts of *hot* water.)
3. Remove the pepper halves, the onion with the cloves, and the bay leaf and discard them. Mash 6 tablespoons of the beans against the side of the pot and stir them into the other beans to make a thick sauce.
4. In a frying pan, sauté chopped green pepper, chopped onion, and garlic in remaining 3 tablespoons olive oil until soft and slightly golden (do not brown); stir mixture into bean pot.
5. Stir the sugar-vinegar mixture into the bean pot.
6. Taste for seasoning, then add salt, if needed.
7. Simmer, uncovered, for 10 minutes. The beans should not be soupy but should have a thick consistency.
8. Serve with rice.

Serves 4 to 6.

Barbecued Butter Beans

Two 14½-ounce cans butter beans
4 tablespoons (½ stick) butter or margarine
1 medium-sized onion, peeled and sliced
1 tablespoon dry mustard
One 10-ounce can tomato soup mixed with 10 ounces water
2 tablespoons Worcestershire sauce
½ teaspoon salt, or to taste
⅓ cup white vinegar
4 to 6 slices lean bacon (optional)

1. Drain the beans, reserving the liquid.
2. In a saucepan, over medium heat, melt the butter or margarine. Add the onion and sauté until it is soft and golden. Do not brown.
3. Stir in the mustard, soup with water, Worcestershire sauce, and salt. Add the liquid from the beans (about 1½ cups). Simmer 5 minutes.
4. Add the vinegar and the beans, stirring. Spoon into a casserole. Cover with the bacon slices.
5. Bake, uncovered, in a preheated 250 F oven for 2 to 3 hours, or until the juice thickens.

Serves 4 to 6.

Chick-peas Creole

You can use canned chick-peas for this interesting side dish.

3 tablespoons butter or margarine
¼ cup finely chopped red or green pepper
3 scallions, white part and small amount of the light green tail, chopped
1 large, ripe tomato, peeled, seeded, chopped, and drained
3 cups cooked chick-peas, drained
Salt and freshly ground black pepper
½ cup grated Gruyère cheese

1. In a saucepan over medium heat, heat half the butter. Add the red or green pepper and scallions and sauté until just soft. Do not brown.
2. Add the tomato and cook 5 minutes. Add the chick-peas, simmering until thoroughly heated through (about 3 minutes).
3. Season with salt and pepper to taste.
4. Stir in the remaining butter and the cheese, heating until melted. Taste for seasoning.

Serves 4 to 6.

Fresh Broad or Fava Beans
Palermo

If fresh fava beans aren't available, the canned or frozen variety are good, too, and much easier to find.

The Beans

3 pounds fresh broad or fava beans in pods, carefully shelled and rinsed
1 large onion, peeled and stuck with 2 whole cloves
2 large celery stalks, each cut into 4 pieces
2 bay leaves
1½ teaspoons salt
Tomato Sauce (recipe follows)
3 tablespoons freshly grated Asiago or Parmesan cheese

1. Half-fill a large deep saucepan with water. Add the beans, onion with cloves, celery, bay leaves, and salt. Over high heat, bring to a boil. Reduce heat, cover, and simmer for 20 minutes, or until the beans are tender.
2. Drain the beans, removing onion, celery, and bay leaves and discarding them. While still hot, stir in several large spoonfuls of the hot tomato sauce. Add more sauce as desired. The beans should be well mixed with the sauce, but should not be over-sauced to a soupy consistency.
3. Sprinkle bean-and-sauce mixture with the freshly grated cheese.

Serves 6.

Tomato Sauce

1 tablespoon butter or margarine
2 tablespoons olive oil
Heaping ¼ cup minced prosciutto or lean bacon

3 large white onions, peeled and finely chopped
6 large fresh basil leaves, minced, or 1 tablespoon dried
¼ teaspoon dried red pepper flakes
6 large ripe tomatoes, peeled and finely chopped
Salt and freshly ground black pepper to taste

1. In a saucepan over medium heat, heat the butter and olive oil. Cook the prosciutto or bacon until crisp but not too brown.
2. Add the onions, basil, and red pepper flakes, simmering and stirring for 6 minutes, or until the onions are soft but not brown.
3. Stir in the tomatoes, salt, and pepper, blending well. Cook, uncovered, for 20 minutes, stirring frequently.
4. This is a light sauce, so raise heat to medium-high and stir and cook just until excess water from the tomatoes has cooked off. Stir frequently. Freeze the unused portion.

Makes approximately 2 cups.

Purée of Fava Beans
Pasquale Limoncelli

This was a favorite of our father and father-in-law, who grew his own fava beans. If you can't find fresh fava beans, fresh limas are a good substitute. Pasquale always served this dish with roast veal and thick-sliced tomatoes from his garden.

5 pounds fresh fava beans in the pod
2 quarts boiling water
3 tablespoons extra virgin olive oil
1 teaspoon salt
Liberal amounts of freshly ground black pepper, or to taste
Light sprinkling of ground mace

1. Shell beans and, with the point of a sharp knife, remove the tough outer skins.
2. Place beans in a pot, cover with boiling water, and simmer over medium heat, covered, for 15 minutes, or until tender. Drain, saving 2 tablespoons of the cooking water.
3. Purée beans in a food mill, blender, or food processor. Spoon the purée into a pot and stir in the reserved 2 tablespoons cooking water. Over low heat, blend in the olive oil and heat, stirring, for 5 minutes, or until the purée is very hot.
4. Sprinkle with salt, pepper, and mace, stirring well. Taste for seasoning. Serve hot.

Serves 4.

Legume Mélange

When assembling the ingredients for the fines herbes, use whatever fresh herbs are available, adding as many or as few as you wish. Dried herbs can be substituted, but you must reduce the total amount to 2 tablespoons.

    1   cup canned white beans
    2   cups fresh peas, shelled
    ½   pound fresh green beans, trimmed and halved
    1   small turnip, scraped and diced
    4   medium-sized carrots, scraped and diced
    ½   cup (1 stick) butter or margarine
    Salt and freshly ground black pepper to taste
    ¼   cup minced fines herbes (fresh chervil, chives, tarragon,
        fennel, parsley, basil, rosemary, thyme, bay leaf)

1. Drain the canned white beans, rinse, and drain again.
2. Cook the peas, green beans, turnip, and carrots in boiling water for 30 minutes, or until tender. They may be cooked separately or together, adding the longer-cooking ones first (turnip, carrots) so that they will all finish cooking at the same time.
3. Drain the vegetables in a colander.
4. Over medium heat, melt the butter or margarine in a saucepan, add the cooked vegetables, then the drained white beans; season with salt and pepper and mix carefully. Simmer for 3 to 4 minutes and blend in the fines herbes. Serve hot.

Serves 4.

Antoine Gilly's
Lentils in Red Wine

Antoine frequently served these lentils with squab, partridge, or quail, but Cornish hen works well, too. He had a dictum: "Do not use an inferior wine for cooking, or the dish may end up inferior."

1½ cups dried lentils
3 tablespoons olive oil
3 large stalks celery, scraped and chopped
3 medium-sized leeks, white part only, thoroughly cleaned and chopped
3 garlic cloves, peeled and chopped
1 teaspoon ground allspice
Salt and freshly ground black pepper to taste
2 cups homemade Chicken Broth (page 13), or canned
1 tablespoon flour
1 cup dry red wine (optional)

1. Pick over the lentils, discarding any foreign material; rinse and drain.
2. In a saucepan over medium heat, heat the olive oil and sauté the celery, leeks, and garlic until just soft. Do not brown.
3. Stir in the allspice, salt, and pepper, then add the lentils. Blend well. Add the chicken broth and bring to a boil over high heat. Cover, reduce heat to low, and simmer for 25 minutes, or until the lentils are just tender.
4. Sprinkle in the flour and add the wine, if desired. Mix gently. Simmer, stirring, for 10 minutes. Taste for seasoning.

Serves 4 to 6.

Lentils with Lemon
Vinaigrette

2 cups dried lentils
½ cup olive oil
4 shallots, peeled and chopped
2 cups homemade Chicken Broth (page 13), or canned
2 tablespoons white vinegar
1 teaspoon salt
½ teaspoon freshly ground black pepper
½ teaspoon sugar
2 tablespoons freshly squeezed lemon juice

1. Pick over lentils, discarding any foreign material, then rinse and drain.
2. In a saucepan over medium heat, heat 2 tablespoons olive oil and cook the shallots for 5 minutes, or just until soft. Do not brown.
3. Place lentils and shallots with their oil in a pot and pour in the chicken broth. Bring to a boil over high heat. Reduce heat to low, cover, and cook for 25 minutes, or until lentils are just soft.
4. Drain the lentils and shallots.
5. Transfer the lentils and shallots to a bowl and let cool.
6. Blend the vinegar, remaining 6 tablespoons olive oil, salt, pepper, and sugar. Pour half of this vinaigrette sauce and the lemon juice over the lentils and blend well.
7. Taste for seasoning, adding more vinaigrette as desired. Serve at room temperature.

Serves 4 to 6.

Bacon-Limas with Tomatoes

5 slices lean bacon, cut into ¼-inch-square pieces
2 small garlic cloves, peeled and minced
6 shallots, peeled and finely chopped
2 tablespoons sherry vinegar
1 teaspoon sugar
4 cups cooked fresh lima beans
2 medium-sized ripe tomatoes, peeled, seeded, cut into
   small cubes, and put in a strainer to drain
Salt and freshly ground black pepper to taste

1. In a deep frying pan over medium heat, cook the bacon until
   golden and crisp. Remove with a slotted spoon and drain on
   paper towels. Reserve.
2. Pour off all but 2 tablespoons of the bacon fat. Add the garlic
   and shallots and sauté until soft but not brown. (Peanut oil may
   be substituted for bacon fat, if desired.)
3. Stir in the vinegar and sugar.
4. Stir in the limas and tomatoes and cook, covered, over medium
   heat until mixture is heated through but the tomatoes are still
   firm.
5. Taste for seasoning, adding salt and pepper as needed.
6. Serve with the crisp bacon squares sprinkled over the top.

Serves 4 to 6.

Navy Beans Burgundy

Burgundian-born chef Antoine Gilly, our mentor, serves broiled French sausages with these beans. We like them just as they are, with warm, crusty French bread.

2 cups dried navy beans
2 tablespoons olive oil
6 shallots, peeled and finely chopped
½ cup dry white wine (optional)
3 very ripe medium-sized tomatoes, peeled, seeded, and chopped
Salt and freshly ground black pepper to taste
3 tablespoons chopped fresh parsley

1. Cover the beans with water and soak for 5 hours. Drain. Alternatively, boil the beans in water for 2 minutes. Remove from heat, cover, and soak for 1 to 2 hours. Drain.
2. Place beans in a large pot and cover with water. Cover pot and cook over low heat for 1½ hours, or until just tender. Drain beans.
3. In a deep saucepan over medium heat, heat the olive oil and cook the shallots for 5 minutes.
4. Stir the wine and tomatoes into the saucepan and bring to a boil over high heat. Immediately turn heat to low and simmer for 15 minutes, stirring. Tomatoes should be soft and just beginning to sauce.
5. Stir in the beans, sprinkling with salt and pepper. Add half the parsley, blending it with the bean mixture. Cover the saucepan and simmer for 10 minutes. Taste for seasoning. Use the remaining parsley to lightly garnish the beans.

Serves 6.

Peas and Cheese Balls

One 16-ounce can tiny peas
2 tablespoons butter or margarine
1 small onion, peeled and finely chopped
1 large egg, beaten
⅓ cup grated Romano cheese
¼ cup fine bread crumbs
¼ teaspoon freshly ground black pepper
2 tablespoons minced fresh parsley
Salt to taste

1. Drain peas and reserve liquid. Set both aside.
2. In a frying pan over medium heat, heat the butter or margarine and sauté the onion until transparent. Do not brown.
3. In a bowl, combine and mix well the onion, egg, cheese, bread crumbs, pepper, and parsley, and form the mixture into balls slightly less than ½ inch in diameter.
4. In a saucepan over medium heat, heat the liquid from the can of peas to a simmer. Add the cheese balls and simmer 4 minutes, shaking the pan occasionally so balls do not stick.
5. Add the peas and heat through.
6. Taste for seasoning, adding salt if needed.

Serves 4.

Maria Limoncelli's
Peas with Chicken

2 tablespoons extra virgin olive oil
2 tablespoons chopped onion
½ boned chicken breast, cut into slightly less than ½-inch cubes
Salt and freshly ground black pepper to taste
One 1-pound can peas, drained, reserving the liquid
¼ cup grated Asiago or Parmesan cheese
1 large egg, well beaten

1. In a saucepan over medium heat, heat the oil. Add the onion and cubed chicken breast and cook about 5 minutes, or until the onion is transparent. Do not brown. Sprinkle lightly with salt and pepper.
2. Add the liquid from the can of peas and simmer 5 minutes.
3. Add the peas and just heat through as the liquid simmers.
4. Just before serving, beat together the cheese and egg; then stir it into the simmering chicken-peas mixture and cook only long enough for the egg to set.
5. Taste for seasoning, and serve immediately.

Serves 4.

Peas with Chicken Broth

An excellent example of how peas not only maintain their own flavor, but magically meld with other flavors. This was a favorite offering of Maria Limoncelli.

3 tablespoons butter or margarine
½ cup homemade Chicken Broth (page 13), or canned
Two 10-ounce packages frozen tiny peas
Salt and freshly ground black pepper to taste
2 tablespoons minced fresh parsley

1. In a saucepan over medium heat, melt the butter or margarine. Add the broth and heat to a simmer. Add the peas, reduce heat, cover, and steam until the peas are tender. Drain.
2. Taste for seasoning, adding salt and pepper if necessary.
3. Add the parsley and serve.

Serves 4 to 6.

Minted Green Peas

Two 10-ounce packages frozen tiny green peas
1 teaspoon sugar
4 tablespoons (½ stick) butter or margarine
2 teaspoons chopped fresh mint leaves
Salt to taste

1. Cook the peas according to package directions, adding the sugar. Undercook slightly. Drain.
2. Place the peas in a saucepan with the butter, mint, and salt. Heat over medium heat. Shake pan well and let stand for 2 minutes, then serve.

Serves 6.

Sweet Peas with Mint and Fresh Mushrooms

Two 10-ounce packages frozen tiny peas
3 tablespoons butter or margarine
¾ pound fresh small mushrooms, washed, dried, and halved
¼ cup sliced almonds
One 10¾-ounce can condensed cream of celery soup
¼ cup water
2 tablespoons chopped pimiento
1 teaspoon fresh chopped mint leaves, or ½ teaspoon crushed dried

1. Cook peas according to package directions, but undercook slightly. Drain and reserve.
2. In a saucepan over medium heat, melt the butter or margarine and cook the mushrooms and almonds for 6 minutes, stirring.
3. Add the remaining ingredients, including the reserved peas, and blend well. Reduce heat and cook, stirring, for 8 minutes.

Serves 6.

Peppered Peas

2 pounds fresh peas (about 2 cups, shelled)
3 tablespoons extra virgin olive oil
1 large onion, peeled and finely chopped
1 medium-sized green pepper, seeded, cored, and cut in strips
1 medium-sized yellow pepper, seeded, cored, and cut in strips
Salt and freshly ground black pepper to taste

1. Simmer peas in lightly salted water until just tender but still firm. Drain well.
2. In a saucepan over medium heat, heat the olive oil and sauté the onion until soft. Do not brown.
3. Add the peppers and simmer, stirring, until soft.
4. Stir in the peas. Season with salt and pepper, and serve.

Serves 4.

Purée of Green Peas

We serve this French classic often, usually with lamb.

> Four 10-ounce packages frozen green peas
> 1 tablespoon sugar
> 9 tablespoons (1 stick plus 1 tablespoon) butter or
>   margarine
> 1 ounce heavy cream or half-and-half
> Salt and freshly ground black pepper to taste
> 2 medium-sized white onions, peeled and thinly sliced

1. Cook the peas according to package directions, adding the sugar.
2. Put the cooked, well-drained peas through a food mill, discarding the skins. Beat the purée with 4 tablespoons butter or margarine, the cream, salt, and pepper until well mixed.
3. Spread the purée evenly in a shallow baking dish.
4. In a frying pan over medium heat, melt 3 tablespoons butter or margarine and cook the onions until soft. Do not brown. Arrange the onions in 6 small mounds on top of the peas. Dot with the remaining 2 tablespoons butter or margarine. Place in a preheated 350 F oven for 20 minutes.

Serves 6.

Tiny Green Peas, Scallions, and Lettuce

Two 10-ounce packages of frozen tiny green peas
1 tablespoon sugar
3 tablespoons finely chopped scallions, white part only
5 tablespoons butter or margarine
1 head Boston lettuce, shredded
Salt and freshly ground black pepper to taste

1. Cook the peas according to package directions, adding the sugar. Undercook slightly. Drain.
2. In a saucepan over medium heat, sauté the scallions in 3 tablespoons butter or margarine until soft. Do not brown. Stir in the lettuce and cook until it has wilted.
3. Add the cooked peas and simmer for 5 minutes, or until the peas are tender.
4. Before serving, stir in the remaining 2 tablespoons butter or margarine and season with salt and pepper.

Serves 4 to 6.

Green Beans with Pine Nuts, Middle Eastern Style

1½ pounds fresh green beans
¼ cup olive oil
2 celery hearts, finely chopped
½ cup pine nuts
2 tablespoons freshly squeezed lemon juice
Salt and freshly ground black pepper to taste
3 tablespoons grated Asiago or Parmesan cheese

1. Cook the green beans in salted boiling water until crisp-tender. Drain well.
2. In a frying pan, heat the olive oil over medium-low heat. Add the celery and pine nuts and cook until the nuts are just golden.
3. Remove from the heat and add the lemon juice, salt, and pepper. Pour the nut mixture over the beans and toss. Taste for seasoning.
4. Serve hot, sprinkling the cheese over individual servings.

Serves 4 to 6.

Green Beans with Mushrooms

2 tablespoons butter or margarine
1 small onion, peeled and finely chopped
1 pound fresh small green beans, trimmed
1 cup sliced small mushrooms
½ cup homemade Chicken Broth (page 13), or canned
Salt and freshly ground black pepper to taste

1. In a saucepan over medium heat, melt the butter or margarine. Add the onion and cook until transparent and soft. Do not brown.
2. Add the beans, mushrooms, and broth and simmer, covered, until the beans are tender. If the broth cooks off before the beans are tender, add a small amount of *hot* broth.
3. Season with salt and pepper.

Serves 4.

Hungarian Green Beans

We had this at a Hungarian restaurant in Vienna, as a side dish offered with a spicy beef stew. Try it with a juicy sirloin or roast chicken.

    3 tablespoons butter or margarine
    1 tablespoon olive oil
    2 medium-sized white onions, peeled and chopped
    1¼ teaspoons sweet Hungarian paprika
    1½ pounds tender young string beans, cut into 1-inch
       pieces
       Salt and freshly ground black pepper to taste
    1 cup water
    1 cup sour cream or plain low-fat yogurt

1. In a deep saucepan over medium heat, heat the butter or margarine and oil and sauté the onions until soft. Do not brown.
2. Add the paprika, string beans, salt, pepper, and water. Bring to a boil, cover, and simmer 15 minutes, or until the beans are crisp-tender. Drain.
3. Stir the sour cream or yogurt into the beans; heat through, stirring. Do not boil.

Serves 4 to 6.

String Bean Savory

1½ pounds small, tender string beans, trimmed and cut
   into 1-inch pieces
6 tablespoons (¾ stick) butter or margarine
¼ pound small fresh mushrooms, cut into ¼-inch-thick
   slices
3 tablespoons flour
2 cups light cream or half-and-half
2 ounces dry sherry (optional)
¾ cup grated Gruyère cheese
Salt and freshly ground black pepper to taste
Bread crumbs

1. Cook the string beans in a small amount of salted boiling water until crisp-tender. Drain thoroughly.
2. In a frying pan over medium heat, melt 2 tablespoons butter or margarine and cook the mushrooms for 2 minutes. Remove with a slotted spoon and reserve.
3. Add 2 more tablespoons butter to the pan. When melted, stir in the flour and cook, stirring into a smooth paste. Gradually add the cream or half-and-half and cook, stirring, blending into a smooth medium-thick sauce. Stir in the sherry, if desired, and add half the cheese, simmering and stirring until the cheese has melted. Season with salt and pepper.
4. Butter a shallow baking dish and arrange the string beans and mushrooms in an even layer. Cover with the sauce. Sprinkle with the remaining cheese, then a thin layer of bread crumbs. Dot with the remaining 2 tablespoons butter or margarine.
5. Cook in a preheated 350 F oven for 20 minutes, or until the sauce is bubbling and the top is golden.

Serves 4 to 6.

Sweet and Sour String Beans

  5 slices very lean bacon, cut into ½-inch pieces (optional)
1½ pounds fresh, tender green string beans
  1 celery stalk, scraped and thinly sliced
  1 small onion, peeled and thinly sliced
  2 tablespoons red wine vinegar
  1 teaspoon sugar
  1 tablespoon Worcestershire sauce
  ¼ teaspoon dry mustard
     Salt to taste

1. Cook the bacon until crisp. Drain, saving the bacon fat.
2. Cook the beans, celery, and onion in lightly salted boiling water until crisp-tender; drain well.
3. Add bacon drippings to the beans and heat through, stirring.
4. In a small nonreactive pan blend the vinegar, sugar, Worcestershire sauce, and mustard, heat through, and pour the mixture over the beans.
5. Add bacon and toss.
6. Taste for seasoning, adding salt, if needed.

Serves 4 to 6.

Puréed Pea Beans

1 pound dried pea or navy beans
4 garlic cloves, peeled and left whole
1 large celery stalk, scraped and halved
2 carrots, scraped and halved
1 medium-sized red pepper, seeded, cored, and quartered
1 teaspoon salt
About 2 cups homemade Chicken Broth (page 13), or
    canned, enough to cover beans
2 tablespoons extra virgin olive oil
½ cup plain low-fat yogurt
Salt and freshly ground black pepper to taste

1. Pick over the beans, discarding any imperfect ones and any foreign material. Soak beans overnight in water, or boil in water
   for 2 minutes, remove from heat, cover, and soak 1 to 2 hours.
   Drain.
2. In a large pot, combine the beans, garlic, celery, carrots, red
   pepper, salt, and broth. Cover pot and bring to a boil. Reduce
   heat to low and simmer for 1½ hours, or until the beans and
   vegetables are tender. Liquid should be absorbed. If not, drain.
3. Transfer cooked beans and vegetables to a blender or food processor and process until smooth but not soupy.
4. Spoon the bean purée into a saucepan. Heat over low heat, stirring, blending in the olive oil and yogurt. Do not boil. Stir in
   salt and pepper to taste. Serve either warm or at room
   temperature.

Serves 6.

Pink Bean Purée

Serve warm in small individual bowls to accompany roast meats.

    2 garlic cloves, peeled and left whole
    3 carrots, scraped and halved
    1 large onion, peeled and halved
    1 teaspoon salt
    Two 16-ounce cans pink beans, drained, rinsed, and
      drained again
    ½ cup dry red wine (optional)
    2 tablespoons extra virgin olive oil
    ¼ teaspoon ground mace
    Salt and freshly ground black pepper to taste

1. In a saucepan, combine the garlic, carrots, onion, and salt. Cover with water and bring to a boil over high heat. Cover pan, reduce heat to medium, and cook until vegetables are tender. Drain and reserve.
2. In a food processor or blender, process the beans into a coarse purée.
3. Add the drained vegetables and red wine, if desired. Process into a smooth but not watery purée.
4. Pour the olive oil into a saucepan, and heat over medium heat. Stir in the bean-vegetable purée, mace, salt, and pepper. Blend well and taste and adjust seasoning. Remove from heat and reserve.
5. Just before serving, simmer the bean purée over medium heat, stirring, until it is hot.

Serves 6.

Baked Light Red
Kidney Bean Casserole

Many of us continue to look for interesting new vegetable dishes or side dishes. Here's a quick and easy one we found in a pleasant restaurant in Reno, Nevada. We like it with broiled chicken.

    2   tablespoons extra virgin olive oil
    1   large onion, peeled and chopped
    2   medium-thick slices Canadian bacon, diced
    1   tablespoon flour
    ½   cup beef broth, homemade or canned
    1   cup dry red wine (optional)
    1   teaspoon salt
    Dash cayenne pepper
    Two 15-ounce cans light red kidney beans, drained, rinsed,
        and drained again

1. In a large saucepan over medium heat, heat the olive oil and sauté the onion until soft. Do not brown. Stir in the Canadian bacon.
2. Sprinkle flour over the onion and bacon. Add the beef broth, wine if using, salt, and cayenne, blending. Simmer 10 minutes.
3. Stir in the light red kidney beans, blending well with the sauce. Spoon into a baking dish or casserole, and place, uncovered, in a preheated 350 F oven for 25 minutes, or until lightly bubbling.

Serves 6.

Speedy Succotash

History credits Native Americans with originating succotash. Immigrants from Europe and elsewhere, long-time legume fans, have added their own strong touches. This dish, for example, was served to us by one of our relatives who came here from the Old World. She used dried beans, but we've turned this into an easy version that nicely fits into today's pressed-for-time life-style. Try this tasty medley as a vegetable side dish to accompany a tender, rosy filet of beef.

One 16-ounce can whole-kernel corn (*not* cream style), drained
One 16-ounce can cannellini beans, drained and rinsed
One 16-ounce can baby lima beans, drained and rinsed
2 tablespoons butter or margarine
Salt and freshly ground black pepper to taste
½ cup heavy cream or half-and-half

1. Combine all ingredients except the cream in a pot, blending well.
2. Heat over medium-high heat, stirring constantly but carefully to avoid breaking up the beans; the dish is almost ready when the butter has melted and blended and the vegetables are hot.
3. Stir in the heavy cream or half-and-half, simmering until thoroughly heated. Do not boil.

Serves 4 to 6.

Spanish Yellow Beans
with Ham

We discovered this recipe at the Palace Hotel in Madrid, a hotel that prided itself on the variety and quality of its menus. We also experienced the Spanish custom of always eating the vegetable offering first. This string bean dish was followed by poached salmon.

1 pound fresh yellow string beans, trimmed
1 tablespoon white vinegar
2 tablespoons extra virgin olive oil
4 shallots, peeled and chopped
¼ cup finely chopped smoked precooked ham
Salt and freshly ground black pepper to taste

1. Over medium-high heat, bring a pot of water to a boil. Add the beans and vinegar.
2. Cook for 3 minutes. Drain; rinse beans in fresh cold water. Drain and dry beans.
3. In a frying pan over medium heat, heat the olive oil and sauté the shallots for 3 minutes, stirring. Do not brown.
4. Add the beans and ham, season with salt and pepper, cover, and simmer over low heat 7 minutes. Beans should be firm but not chewy.

Serves 4.

6

Side Dishes

Why aren't side dishes part of the vegetable chapter? Because we consider them special parts of a meal. Legumes, yes, but with a creative difference, offering a remarkable variety of taste trends.

These side dishes are so satisfying, in fact, that in today's "eat light" society, guests might be confused and mistake some of them for main courses.

That *would* be a mistake, especially if you follow some of our suggestions and offer Yellow String Beans Tetrazzini with tender, juicy broiled chicken, or Lentils with Bulgur Wheat with that Middle Eastern lamb delicacy, shish kebab, or Chick-peas and Chicken Livers Risotto with swordfish steaks.

There are exciting dishes ahead: The rousing Mexico City Pink Beans, Shirley Capp's Baby Green Beans, Bacon, and Potatoes, and Clara Darcangelo's mashed-and-whole-bean Italian treat, Beans and Cabbage.

Clara M. Darcangelo's
Beans and Cabbage

Puréeing half the beans makes this dish especially creamy. Our friend Clara, one of the cleverest of cooks, originated this dish.

6 tablespoons olive oil
1 large garlic clove, peeled and minced
¼ cup finely diced carrots
¼ cup finely diced celery
½ cup finely diced peeled onions
1 teaspoon chopped fresh parsley
½ teaspoon chopped fresh basil, or ¼ teaspoon dried
1 smoked ham hock (optional)
2 cups tomato sauce
2 quarts plus 1 cup water
1 teaspoon salt
½ teaspoon freshly ground black pepper
1 pound dried white beans, soaked 5 hours or quick-soaked (see page 10)
1 whole medium-sized onion, peeled
One 2- to 2¼-pound head of cabbage, cored, trimmed and coarsely chopped

1. In a large pot over medium heat, heat 3 tablespoons olive oil. Add the garlic, carrots, celery, diced onion, parsley, basil, and ham hock. Cook until vegetables are golden. Do not brown.
2. Add the tomato sauce, 1 quart water, salt, and pepper and simmer about 1 hour, or until the hock is about half-cooked.
3. Add the drained beans, the whole onion, and the remaining 5 cups water, and simmer until the beans are almost cooked.
4. Discard the whole onion, and purée half the beans. Return the purée to the bean pot.
5. Meanwhile, in another pot over medium heat, heat the remain-

ing 3 tablespoons olive oil and simmer the cabbage, covered, until partially cooked.

6. Stir the cabbage into the bean pot and simmer until the cabbage is tender. Taste for seasoning, and serve on a warm platter.

Serves 6.

Chick-peas and
Chicken Livers Risotto

We like to serve this Italian preparation with broiled swordfish steaks.

    3 tablespoons extra virgin olive oil
    1 medium-sized onion, peeled and chopped
    6 chicken livers, each cut into 8 pieces
    6 medium-sized mushrooms, quartered
    Salt to taste
    ⅓ cup dry white wine (optional)
    One 15-ounce can chick-peas, drained, rinsed, and drained
        again
    3½ cups homemade Chicken Broth (page 13), or canned
    2 cups long-grain converted rice
    2 tablespoons chopped fresh parsley
    1 cup grated Asiago or Parmesan cheese

1. In a large frying pan over medium heat, heat the olive oil and
   sauté onion 4 minutes. Add the livers and cook 2 minutes.
2. Add the mushrooms, sprinkling mushrooms and livers lightly
   with salt. Stir in the wine, if using, and the chick-peas. Cook over
   medium heat 3 minutes, stirring.
3. In a pot over medium-high heat, heat the chicken broth until
   bubbling. Stir in the rice, cover, reduce heat to low, and cook
   20 minutes, or until rice is just tender.
4. Add the chicken liver and mushroom mixture to the rice pot
   and stir. Add the parsley, toss well, fluffing up the rice with 2
   forks. Taste for seasoning.
5. With a fork, carefully stir in ½ cup grated cheese. Sprinkle
   remaining cheese over individual servings of the risotto, which
   should be slightly moist.

Serves 6.

Chick-peas, New Potatoes, and Swiss Chard

If you are pressed for time, use 3 cups of canned chick-peas, rinsed and drained, instead of the dried. Add them at the end with the potatoes and chard.

1 cup dried chick-peas
12 to 18 tiny new potatoes, unpeeled
¾ pound Swiss chard, coarsely chopped (first remove the coarse center rib)
1 cup homemade Chicken Broth (page 13), or canned
2 tablespoons butter or margarine
1 medium-sized onion, peeled and chopped
1 garlic clove, peeled and minced
3 large ripe tomatoes, peeled, seeded, and chopped
Pinch dried red pepper flakes (optional)
Pinch dried oregano
1 teaspoon sugar
Salt to taste

1. Wash the chick-peas well. Soak overnight well covered with water. Drain, place in a saucepan, and cover with water. Bring to a boil, reduce heat and simmer 2½ hours, or until tender, adding more *hot* water if needed. Or, to soak more quickly, place chick-peas in a saucepan, cover with 2 inches of water, boil 2 minutes, remove from heat, and let stand, covered, for 2 hours. Bring to a boil and simmer until tender, adding more *hot* water, if needed. Drain and reserve.
2. Boil the potatoes in their skins until tender, drain and dry over heat in the pan. Set aside.
3. Cook the Swiss chard in the chicken broth until tender. Drain, saving the broth. Set Swiss chard aside.
4. In a large frying pan, heat the butter or margarine and sauté the onion and garlic for about 2 minutes, or until soft. Do not brown. Add the reserved chard broth, the tomatoes, red pepper

flakes, oregano, sugar, and salt. Simmer, uncovered, for 15 minutes, or until sauce has thickened.

5. While the sauce simmers, remove a band of skin from the center third of the potatoes, leaving the skin on both ends.
6. Stir into the sauce the chick-peas, potatoes, and chard and simmer 5 minutes, or until heated through. Taste for seasoning and serve.
7. Pass grated Asiago or Parmesan cheese at the table.

Serves 4 to 6.

Shirley Capp's Baby Green Beans, Potatoes, and Bacon

For this recipe to work, you must have your own garden, or know of a store that carries only the freshest produce. The green beans must be baby ones, twice the thickness of matchsticks; the potatoes must be new ones, smaller than walnuts.

> 6 slices lean bacon
> 24 tiny new potatoes, unpeeled
> 1 pound baby green beans, trimmed
> Salt and freshly ground black pepper to taste

1. In a large frying pan or saucepan, cook the bacon until crisp. Drain on paper towels, and break bacon into ¼-inch pieces. Set aside. Save the bacon fat in its pan.
2. Wash the new potatoes well, leaving most of the moisture on them. Place them in the pan with the bacon fat (or use vegetable oil if you prefer), cover, and cook 5 minutes.
3. Rinse the green beans, leaving most of the moisture on them, and add them to the pan with the potatoes. Cover and cook over medium heat, shaking the pan occasionally, until both are tender, and the beans still slightly crisp. If you don't have enough moisture to cook until tender, add small amounts of *hot* water.
4. Before serving, stir in the bacon and cook, covered, for 2 minutes to heat through. Season with salt and pepper.

Serves 4.

Kedgeree

1½ cups dried lentils
5 cups water
2 teaspoons salt
1 cup rice
3 tablespoons butter or margarine
½ teaspoon ground cumin
Pinch ground cardamom seed (about ⅛ teaspoon)
Pinch ground coriander (about ⅛ teaspoon)
Pinch turmeric (about ⅛ teaspoon)
3 whole cloves
¼ teaspoon freshly ground black pepper

1. Pick over the lentils, discarding any foreign material. Rinse and drain.
2. In a saucepan, bring the water with the salt to a boil. Add the rice and lentils. Reduce heat and cook, covered, for 20 minutes, or until most of the liquid has cooked off and the rice and lentils are very soft. If liquid cooks off before the rice and lentils are cooked, add a *small* amount of *hot* water. The consistency of the mixture should be fairly dry.
3. In a small frying pan, heat the butter or margarine. Stir in the cumin, cardamom, coriander, turmeric, cloves, and pepper, blending well. Add this mixture to the rice and lentils and blend well. Taste for seasoning. Remove and discard cloves (if you can find them).

Serves 4 to 6.

Legumes and Escarole
Casserole

3 heads escarole, trimmed and thoroughly washed under
    running water
¼ cup olive oil
3 garlic cloves, peeled and minced
½ teaspoon dried oregano
4 thin slices salami, diced (optional)
2 cups hot homemade Chicken Broth (page 13), or canned
One 16-ounce can pinto beans, drained, rinsed, and
    drained again
One 10-ounce package frozen baby limas, cooked
    according to package directions
Salt and freshly ground black pepper to taste

1. In a large pot, blanch the escarole in salted boiling water for 4
   minutes. Drain and chop coarsely.
2. Add the olive oil and garlic to the pot used to cook the lettuce.
   Sauté over medium heat, just until garlic is soft, about 3 minutes. Do not brown.
3. Stir in the oregano and salami and cook for 2 minutes. Add the
   escarole and the chicken broth. Cover the pot and cook over
   medium heat for 10 minutes, or until the escarole is just tender.
4. Stir in the pinto beans and limas, salt, and pepper (taste before
   adding salt, as the broth may have supplied enough) and cook 5
   minutes, or until the beans are thoroughly heated.

Serves 6.

Legume Risotto

We discovered this colorful party dish in a trattoria in Rome. Try serving it with roast chicken.

    ¼ cup extra virgin olive oil
    3 large carrots, scraped and diced
    1½ cups long-grain converted rice
    4 cups beef broth, homemade or canned
One 10-ounce package frozen tiny peas, partially defrosted
One 10-ounce package frozen baby lima beans, partially
        defrosted
One 10-ounce package frozen sliced green beans, partially
        defrosted
    1 teaspoon salt
    ¼ teaspoon dried red pepper flakes, or to taste
    1 cup grated Asiago or Parmesan cheese

1. In a large deep saucepan over medium heat, heat the olive oil and cook the carrots, stirring, for 4 minutes.
2. Stir in the rice. In another pot, bring the beef broth to a boil, and add it to the rice and carrots.
3. Add the peas, limas, and sliced green beans, stirring them into the rice mixture. Season with salt and red pepper flakes, stirring to blend.
4. Cover the saucepan and bring mixture to a boil over high heat. Reduce heat and simmer the legume risotto for 20 minutes.
5. Remove from heat and stir in half the grated cheese, blending it with the rice and vegetables. Toss the risotto, fluffing it up with 2 forks. It should be slightly moist. Taste for seasoning. Pass the remaining cheese at the table.

Serves 6 to 8.

Lentils with Bulgur Wheat

Serve this with shish kebab for a nice melding of Middle Eastern favorites.

> 2 cups dried lentils
> 2 large onions, peeled and chopped
> ⅓ cup olive oil
> 5 cups water
> Salt
> 1 cup bulgur wheat
> 2 tablespoons soft butter or margarine
> 1 cup chopped fresh broad-leaf parsley
> ½ cup chopped scallions, white part only
> Freshly ground black pepper to taste

1. Pick over the lentils, discarding any foreign material, and rinse them well.
2. In a frying pan over medium heat, sauté the onions in the olive oil until golden. Do not brown.
3. In a saucepan, simmer the lentils in the water with 1 teaspoon salt for 15 minutes, or until just cooked, not mushy.
4. Add the cooked onions and any oil in the pan, the bulgur wheat, and 1 tablespoon parsley to the lentils and stir. Cover and simmer over low heat for 15 minutes. Let lentils and bulgur wheat absorb the liquid. Stir in the butter or margarine. Taste for seasoning, adding pepper and more salt, if needed.
5. Cool slightly, then shape into patties and arrange on a hot platter, garnishing with the scallions and remaining parsley. Serve warm.

Serves 6.

Lentil Pilaf

In Istanbul this dish was served to us with slices of spicy roast lamb.

> 1 cup dried lentils
> 2 cups water
> Salt
> 2½ cups homemade Chicken Broth (page 13), or canned
> 1 cup long-grain converted rice
> 2 tablespoons extra virgin olive oil
> 4 shallots, peeled and chopped
> 2 celery stalks, scraped and chopped

1. Pick over the lentils, discarding any foreign material. Rinse and drain. In a saucepan, bring 2 cups of water and 1 teaspoon salt to a boil over medium-high heat. Add the lentils and cook 3 minutes. Drain.
2. In the same pan, bring the chicken broth to a boil, reduce heat to low, and add the lentils and the rice. Season with salt and stir to blend. Cover the pan and simmer for 20 minutes, or until lentils and rice are tender but not mushy and liquid is absorbed. (If liquid is absorbed before lentils and rice are tender, add a small amount of hot broth.) Remove from heat.
3. In a frying pan over medium heat, heat the olive oil and cook the shallots and celery until soft, but do not brown.
4. Add the shallots and celery to the lentil and rice mixture. Fluff up with a fork to blend, over medium heat. Taste for seasoning.

Serves 4 to 6.

Limas Luisa

1 pound dried lima beans
4 tablespoons (½ stick) butter or margarine
1 large onion, peeled and chopped
1 sweet red pepper, seeded, trimmed, and chopped
One 10-ounce can tomato soup
1¼ cups homemade Chicken Broth (page 13), or canned
Salt and freshly ground black pepper to taste
6 slices lean bacon, cooked until golden brown and crisp, drained on paper towels, and coarsely chopped (optional)

1. Pick over beans, discarding any foreign material and imperfect beans. Rinse and drain.
2. Place beans in a saucepan, cover with water, bring to a boil, and boil 2 minutes. Remove from heat, cover, and soak 1 hour. Return to heat and simmer beans 1 hour, or until just tender but still intact. Add more hot water, if needed. Drain the beans.
3. In a deep frying pan, melt the butter or margarine. Add the onion and red pepper and cook until soft. Do not brown.
4. Stir the tomato soup into the beans. Add chicken broth and salt and pepper. Stir in the onion-pepper mixture. Taste for seasoning.
5. Blend all well and pour into a 2-quart casserole. Cook in a 350 F oven 45 minutes, or until the top is golden brown and the liquid bubbling. Sprinkle the bacon over the top.

Serves 4 to 6.

Neapolitan Limas

2 tablespoons olive oil
1 medium-sized onion, peeled and chopped
1 garlic clove, peeled and minced
1 small green pepper, seeded, cored, and chopped
4 large ripe tomatoes, peeled, seeded, and chopped
3 pounds fresh lima beans, shelled
Salt and freshly ground black pepper to taste
½ teaspoon sugar
¼ cup homemade Chicken Broth (page 13), or canned

1. Heat the oil in a saucepan over medium heat. Add the onion, garlic, and green pepper and sauté until onion is soft, about 3 minutes. Do not brown.
2. Add the tomatoes, beans, salt, pepper, sugar, and chicken broth and simmer, uncovered, until the beans are tender and the sauce thickens, about 15 minutes. If sauce thickens before beans are tender, add a small amount of *hot* stock.

Serves 4.

Baby Lima Beans with Rice and Pimiento

2 tablespoons butter or margarine
⅛ teaspoon ground sage
½ teaspoon salt
½ cup long-grain converted rice
1 cup homemade Chicken Broth (page 13), or canned
2 tablespoons diced pimiento
One 10-ounce package frozen baby limas, cooked
   according to package directions and drained

1. In a deep saucepan over high heat, melt the butter or margarine. Stir in the sage and salt, and blend in the rice.
2. Pour in the chicken broth. When it is boiling, cover the pan, reduce heat to low, and simmer for 20 minutes, or until rice is tender and liquid is absorbed.
3. Stir in the pimiento and limas and heat through, blending well.

Serves 4.

Creamed Fresh Peas with Potatoes

This is a dish traditionally served with fresh poached whole salmon or with grilled or sautéed salmon steaks. We also like to serve it with salmon loaf or salmon patties made from canned salmon.

1 pound young, fresh peas, shelled (about 1 cup shelled), or 1 cup frozen tiny peas
4 medium-sized new potatoes
1 cup heavy cream or half-and-half
½ cup milk
Salt and freshly ground black pepper to taste
⅛ teaspoon mace
⅛ teaspoon sugar

1. Cook the peas in boiling salted water until just tender, and drain thoroughly. If using frozen peas, cook according to package directions. Set aside.
2. Boil the potatoes in their skins until barely tender, drain, and dry over heat in the pan. Peel and cut into ¼-inch-thick slices.
3. In a saucepan, combine the potatoes, cream or half-and-half, and milk. Bring just to a simmer. Season with salt, pepper, and mace. Sprinkle in the sugar and stir carefully, in order not to break up the potatoes. Simmer for 6 minutes.
4. While the potatoes and sauce are still simmering, stir in the peas and taste for seasoning.

Serves 4.

Curried Peas and Potatoes

6 medium-sized potatoes
2 tablespoons vegetable oil
1 medium-sized onion, peeled and finely chopped
1 teaspoon curry powder
1 teaspoon grated fresh ginger
¼ cup tomato purée
½ cup hot water
One 10-ounce package frozen tiny peas, defrosted
Salt to taste
1 cup plain low-fat yogurt

1. Cook the potatoes in their skins in boiling water until tender, drain, and dry over heat in the pan. Peel and cut into bite-sized pieces. Set aside.
2. In a large saucepan over medium heat, heat the oil and cook the onion for 1 minute, or until it is soft. Do not brown. Stir in the curry powder and ginger. Cook 1 minute.
3. Mix the tomato purée with the hot water, stir it into the onions, and simmer, uncovered, until sauce starts to thicken.
4. Add the peas and simmer until just tender. Add the potatoes, salt, and yogurt and cook until heated through. Do not boil.

Serves 6.

Pea Bean Pudding

2 cups dried pea beans
1 tablespoon molasses
1½ teaspoons Dijon mustard
1 tablespoon extra virgin olive oil
1 tablespoon balsamic vinegar
3 tablespoons freshly squeezed lemon juice
Salt and freshly ground black pepper to taste

1. Pick over the beans, discarding any foreign material and imperfect beans. Rinse and drain. Cover the beans with cold water, bring the water to a boil, reduce heat, and simmer, covered, for 1 to 1½ hours, or until the beans are tender. Drain.
2. In a food processor or blender, purée the cooked beans.
3. Transfer the purée to a saucepan and stir in the molasses, mustard, oil, vinegar, lemon juice, salt, and pepper. Reheat over low heat just before serving, being careful not to burn.

Serves 6 to 8.

Pink Beans au Gratin

1 pound dried pink beans
Salt and freshly ground black pepper to taste
1 onion, peeled and stuck with 1 whole clove
Bouquet garni (1 sprig thyme, broad-leaf parsley, and 1
    bay leaf, tied in a piece of cheesecloth)
1 garlic clove, peeled and mashed
¼ pound blanched bacon (optional)
4 tablespoons (½ stick) butter or margarine
¼ cup grated Swiss cheese
¼ cup fine dry bread crumbs

1. Pick over the beans, discarding any foreign material and imperfect beans. Rinse and drain. Soak the beans in water to cover 8
   to 12 hours; or boil in water 2 minutes, remove from heat,
   cover, and soak 1 to 2 hours.
2. Drain the beans. Place them in a saucepan and cover with cold
   water. Bring to a boil, add salt, pepper, the cloved onion, bouquet garni, garlic, and blanched bacon. Cover the pan and simmer over low heat 30 minutes, or until the beans are tender.
   Taste for seasoning.
3. Remove and discard the onion, bouquet garni, garlic, and
   bacon. Drain any remaining liquid. The beans should be well
   drained.
4. Use part of the butter or margarine to butter a baking dish. Add
   the beans in one level layer. Dot with the remaining butter or
   margarine. Sprinkle with the cheese and bread crumbs, and
   bake in a preheated 375 F oven for 20 minutes, or until golden.

Serves 4.

Mexico City Pink Beans

These powerful beans were first served to us with grilled fish in Mexico City. Serrano chiles are green and have a fresh, strong flavor. The seeds and veins of serranos, however, are fiery. Handle them carefully, washing your hands immediately after washing and chopping the peppers. Or wear gloves. (If you want to play it safe, use sweet green peppers.) We substitute hot Italian-style turkey sausage for the pork rind and bacon in the original Mexican recipe.

1½ cups dried pink beans
½ pound hot Italian-style turkey sausage, cut into ¼-inch slices
1 medium-sized onion, peeled and thinly sliced
2 garlic cloves, peeled and finely chopped
2 teaspoons salt
2 tablespoons olive oil
2 large, ripe tomatoes, peeled, seeded, and chopped
2 small serrano chiles, stemmed, seeded, and finely chopped
¾ teaspoon ground coriander

1. Place the beans, sausage, onion, and garlic in a pot, adding 8 cups of water. Bring to a boil. Cover pot, reduce heat to low, and simmer beans gently for 1½ hours, or until they are just tender.
2. Stir in the salt and simmer, uncovered, for 20 minutes.
3. In a saucepan, heat the olive oil over low heat, and cook the tomatoes, chiles, and coriander for 10 minutes, uncovered, stirring. Raise heat and cook 10 minutes, until the tomato-pepper mixture is fairly thick.
4. Stir the tomato-pepper mixture into the bean pot and cook, stirring occasionally (and gently), over low heat for 15 minutes.

Serves 6.

Spicy Pintos

The final slow cooking, western style, produces a rich, flavorful brown sauce. Provide warm thick slices of bread for dunking.

    1 pound dried pinto beans
    2 medium-sized onions, peeled and chopped
    2 garlic cloves, peeled and finely chopped
    1 bay leaf
    1 teaspoon salt
    ½ pound smoked ham, cut into ½-inch cubes
    One 16-ounce can tomatoes, including liquid
    1 small green pepper, seeded, cored, and chopped
    2 tablespoons brown sugar
    2 teaspoons chili powder
    ½ teaspoon dry mustard
    ½ teaspoon ground cumin

1. Pick over the beans, discarding any foreign material and imperfect beans. Rinse and drain.
2. Place beans in a saucepan and add enough water to cover beans by 1 inch. Bring to a boil. Boil 2 minutes, remove from heat, cover, and let stand 1 hour. Drain beans. Cover with fresh water.
3. Add the onions, garlic, bay leaf, salt, and ham to the bean pot and, over medium-high heat, bring to a boil. Reduce heat to low, cover pot, and simmer 1½ hours. Beans should not be thoroughly cooked but remain slightly firm. If water cooks off, add more hot water to barely cover beans. Stir occasionally.
4. Break up the tomatoes in a bowl and add them and the green pepper, brown sugar, chili powder, mustard, and cumin to the bean pot. Stir.
5. Transfer mixture to a casserole. Place in a 300 F oven and bake for 4 hours, or until the beans are tender and the sauce is

medium-thick. If the sauce seems to be cooking off before the beans are tender, cover casserole with aluminum foil.
6. Remove and discard bay leaf. Taste for seasoning.

Note: This dish can also be cooked very slowly on top of the stove, but it should be stirred occasionally to prevent burning. It doesn't have to be watched so closely in the oven.

Serves 4 to 6.

Red Bean Medley

 2 cups canned red kidney beans, drained, rinsed, and
    drained again
 1 cup canned chick-peas, drained, rinsed, and drained
    again
1½ cups homemade Chicken Broth (page 13), or canned
 2 medium-sized ripe tomatoes, peeled, seeded, and
    chopped
 ½ cup trimmed chopped scallions
 ½ cup finely chopped fresh basil
 ½ cup extra virgin olive oil
    Juice of 2 medium-sized lemons
1½ teaspoons salt

1. Place the kidney beans, chick-peas, and chicken broth in a sauce-pan and heat over medium heat, stirring, until warm. Drain liquid.
2. While the beans and chick-peas are still warm, place them in a large bowl. Add the tomatoes, scallions, and basil.
3. Meanwhile, in another small bowl, blend well the olive oil, lemon juice, and salt.
4. Spoon this dressing over the beans mixture, blending well. Taste for seasoning. Serve at room temperature.

Serves 4.

Split Pea Curry
with Vegetables

¼ cup light olive oil
1 medium-sized onion, peeled and chopped
2 garlic cloves, peeled and minced
1 tablespoon curry powder
1 teaspoon ground cumin
1 cup dried yellow split peas, picked over, rinsed, and
   drained
3 cups water
3 tablespoons freshly squeezed lemon juice
1 teaspoon salt
½ teaspoon freshly ground black pepper
1 small eggplant, peeled and cut into ½-inch cubes
1 small cauliflower, cut into florets
½ cup raisins
½ cup shredded coconut
¼ cup chopped fresh parsley

1. In a pan large enough to hold all ingredients, heat the oil over
   medium heat and cook the onion, garlic, curry, and cumin for
   10 minutes, or until the onion is just tender. Do not brown.
2. Stir in the split peas, water, lemon juice, salt, and pepper. Cover
   pan and bring to a boil over low heat. Simmer 15 minutes.
3. Add the eggplant, cauliflower, and raisins. Simmer over low
   heat, covered, for 20 minutes, or until vegetables are tender.
   Stir in the coconut and parsley and serve immediately.

Serves 8.

Split Peas with Eggplant

2 cups dried split green or yellow peas
1 onion, peeled and chopped
1 teaspoon salt
½ teaspoon cayenne
3 tablespoons peanut oil
1 teaspoon cumin seed
½ teaspoon mustard seed
2 small eggplants, peeled and cut into ½-inch cubes
2 medium-sized potatoes, cut into ½-inch cubes

1. Pick over the peas, discarding any foreign material and imperfect peas. Rinse well and drain.
2. In a saucepan, cover the peas with cold water. Add the onion, salt, and cayenne. Cover, bring to a boil, reduce heat to medium-low, and cook 20 minutes, or until the peas are slightly underdone. Drain the peas, saving the liquid.
3. In a deep frying pan, heat the peanut oil. Add the cumin and mustard seeds and cook until the mustard seeds pop.
4. Add the peas to the pan with the cumin and mustard seeds, along with the eggplant and potatoes. Add enough of the reserved cooking liquid to barely cover all ingredients. If not enough to cover, add water. Cover, and simmer over medium heat until vegetables and peas are tender, about 15 minutes. Taste for seasoning.

Serves 4 to 6.

Green Split Pea Curry

  1 cup green split peas
  2 cups beef broth, homemade or canned
  1 teaspoon curry powder
  ¼ teaspoon turmeric
  ½ teaspoon paprika
  1 medium-sized red onion, peeled and chopped
  1 garlic clove, peeled and minced
Salt and freshly ground black pepper to taste

1. Pick over peas, removing any foreign material, rinse well, and drain. Place peas in a pot and add the beef broth.
2. Stir in the curry powder, turmeric, paprika, onion, and garlic. Season lightly with salt and pepper, blending well. Cover pot and simmer for 30 minutes, or until the peas are tender.
3. Serve the pea curry spooned over individual portions of rice.

Serves 4.

Soybean Casserole

Dried soybeans are not very easy to find. Look for them in natural-food shops.

This dish goes well with lean roast pork.

> 1½ cups dried soybeans
> 4 shallots, peeled and chopped
> 4 slices thick-sliced lean bacon, diced (optional)
> ½ cup chili sauce
> 1 teaspoon salt
> 1 tablespoon brown sugar
> 1 teaspoon dry mustard
> ¼ cup Madeira wine (optional)

1. Pick over beans, discarding any foreign material and imperfect beans. Rinse well and drain. Soak in water to cover overnight; or boil in water to cover for 2 minutes, remove from heat, cover, and soak 1 to 2 hours. Drain.
2. Place beans in a deep saucepan, cover with water, bring to a boil, reduce heat to low, and simmer, covered, for 3 hours, or until the soybeans are tender. Drain.
3. In a casserole, combine the beans, shallots, bacon, chili sauce, salt, brown sugar, dry mustard, and Madeira, blending well.
4. Cover the casserole and bake in a preheated 350 F oven for 25 minutes.
5. Remove cover, stir beans well, reduce heat to 300 F and cook 25 minutes longer, or until the sauce has thickened.

Serves 4.

Yellow String Beans
Tetrazzini

This appealing dish—an out-of-the-ordinary vegetable—goes especially well with chicken, and holds up well as a leftover.

2 pounds small fresh yellow string beans, trimmed
4 tablespoons (½ stick) butter or margarine, plus
   additional to top dish
¼ pound fresh mushrooms, cut into ¼-inch slices
3 tablespoons flour
2 cups cream or half-and-half
2 ounces dry sherry (optional)
¾ cup grated fontina or Gruyère cheese
Salt and freshly ground black pepper to taste
Unseasoned bread crumbs

1. Simmer the string beans, covered, in boiling salted water 15 minutes, or until just crisp-tender (they will cook a little more later). Drain. Cut into 1-inch pieces.
2. In a saucepan over medium heat, melt 1 tablespoon butter or margarine, and sauté the mushrooms for 3 minutes. Remove mushrooms with a slotted spoon and reserve.
3. Add the remaining 3 tablespoons butter or margarine to the saucepan. Melt over medium heat and stir in the flour. Cook, stirring into a smooth paste.
4. Gradually add the cream and cook, stirring, into a smooth medium-thick sauce. Stir in the sherry and ½ cup cheese and cook, stirring, over low heat, until the cheese has melted. Season with salt and pepper to taste.
5. Arrange the string beans and mushrooms in a shallow buttered baking dish. Spoon the cheese sauce over them, and sprinkle with the remaining cheese. Sprinkle lightly with bread crumbs and dot with butter or margarine. Bake on center rack position, uncovered, in a preheated 350 F oven for 20 minutes, or until the sauce is bubbling and the top is golden.

Serves 6.

❧ 7 ❧

Main Dishes

In this chapter you'll find some of our favorite legume dishes combined with fish, meat, and poultry to make satisfying and delicious main-dish meals. We've also included here some new low-fat recipes featuring chicken and turkey sausages and ground turkey.

Besides our old favorites, such as Peas and Chicken Pilaf and Snow Peas, Bean Sprouts, and Chicken Breasts, Chinese Style, we offer new and unique main-dish ideas, including White Kidney and Fava Beans with Braised Lamb Shanks, Green Beans with Scallops, Chick-peas with Macaroni, and Cannellini Beans with Pesto and Chicken Scaloppine Marsala.

It's here that you find, too, the great classic legume recipes, such as Cassoulet à la Paysanne and Boston Baked Beans. These are tried-and-true dishes that have survived the test of time. Each one is presented in its original version, using traditional ingredients. If you prefer, substitute other ingredients in place of salt pork or fatback, for example, but be warned: The taste will not be quite the same.

Black or Pinto Beans with Chicken, Southwestern Style

¼ cup olive oil
One 3½-pound chicken, cut up
Salt and freshly ground black pepper to taste
1 large onion, peeled and chopped
1 sweet red pepper, seeded, deribbed, and chopped
1 small fresh jalapeño pepper, seeded and chopped
2 garlic cloves, peeled and minced
1 teaspoon ground cumin
1 large ripe tomato, peeled and chopped
1 tablespoon freshly squeezed lemon juice
One 15-ounce can black or pinto beans, drained, rinsed, and drained again

1. In a large frying pan over medium-high heat, heat the olive oil. Add the chicken, sprinkle lightly with salt and pepper, and cook 5 minutes. Turn chicken over and cook an additional 5 minutes. Chicken should be golden brown. Remove from pan.
2. In the pan in which the chicken cooked, over medium heat, add the onion, red pepper, jalapeño, and garlic (add more oil if needed). Sauté, stirring, 5 minutes, or until the onions are soft. Do not brown.
3. Stir in cumin, tomato, lemon juice, and beans. Add the browned chicken, mixing with the vegetables, cover, and simmer over medium-low heat for 20 minutes. Remove cover and cook 10 minutes more, or until chicken is tender. Taste for seasoning. Serve with sauce spooned over individual servings of chicken, accompanied by hot rice.

Serves 4.

Black Bean Sauce with Shrimp

Our friend Wah Chin introduced us to this dish several years ago. We were so taken with it that he invited us to his home the following evening and demonstrated its preparation.

2 heaping tablespoons Chinese fermented black beans (available in gourmet and oriental food shops), rinsed in fresh cold water several times to remove excess saltiness and well drained
2 garlic cloves, peeled and minced
1 tablespoon peanut oil
1 tablespoon soy sauce
1 tablespoon dry sherry (optional)
1 teaspoon sugar
One 14-ounce can clear chicken broth
4 thin slices fresh ginger
3 tablespoons water
1 tablespoon cornstarch
32 medium-sized shrimp, shelled, deveined, simmered in boiling water just until pink, and drained

1. Use a mortar and pestle, food processor, or blender to make a paste of the beans and garlic. *Don't* overprocess into a watery paste.
2. In a large frying pan or wok over medium-high heat, heat the peanut oil and stir-fry the bean paste for 30 seconds.
3. Combine the soy sauce, sherry, and sugar, and add them to the pan with the bean paste, blending. Stir for 30 seconds over medium-high heat.
4. Stir in the chicken broth and ginger. Bring to a boil. Blend the water and cornstarch together, and add them to the pan, stirring and blending the mixture until smooth and thick.
5. Arrange 8 shrimp on each of 4 warm plates. Spoon the bean sauce over the shrimp, and serve with generous mounds of rice.

Serves 4.

Black Beans with
Chicken Sates

Here's a unique combination of Latin and Eastern cultures that should intrigue your dinner guests.

Beans

2 tablespoons extra virgin olive oil
4 shallots, peeled and chopped
Juice of ½ lemon
1 teaspoon salt
½ teaspoon freshly ground black pepper
½ teaspoon dried marjoram
Two 16-ounce cans black beans (labeled "frijoles negros" in some markets), drained, rinsed, and drained again

1. Heat the olive oil over medium heat in a saucepan. Sauté the shallots 5 minutes, or until soft. Do not brown.
2. Add the lemon juice, salt, pepper, and marjoram. Stir in the beans, blending well but carefully. Taste for seasoning. Reserve.

Sates

⅓ cup peanut oil
6 tablespoons freshly squeezed lime juice, strained
½ teaspoon ground ginger
2 teaspoons ground coriander
Salt and freshly ground black pepper to taste
3 whole boned chicken breasts, cut into 1½ inch cubes
1 cup shredded coconut, toasted

1. In a deep bowl, combine and blend well the peanut oil, lime juice, ginger, coriander, salt, and pepper.

2. Add the chicken pieces, blending well with the marinade to coat thoroughly. Marinate for 2 or more hours at room temperature.
3. Thread the chicken pieces on skewers. Broil in center portion of oven 3 minutes.
4. Turn chicken, brush with marinade, broil another 3 minutes.
5. Turn chicken, brushing with marinade. Broil 3 minutes longer. Be careful in the broiling, testing the chicken at least twice with a sharp fork. It should not be overdone.
6. Place coconut in a flat plate. Dredge the cooked chicken pieces with the coconut to coat well.
7. Gently reheat beans and serve with the hot chicken.

Serves 4 to 6.

Cannellini Beans with Pesto
and Chicken Scaloppine
Marsala

Italians like beans almost as much as they like pasta, and so they sometimes combine their classic pasta sauces with legumes. This dish is a tasty example.

Beans

Two 16-ounce cans cannellini beans (labeled "white kidney beans" in some markets)

Drain the beans, rinse thoroughly, and drain again. Set aside.

Pesto Sauce

2 cups fresh basil leaves, washed and dried
½ cup fresh broad-leaf parsley, washed and dried
½ cup plus 2 tablespoons grated Asiago or Parmesan cheese
½ cup grated Romano cheese
14 shelled walnut halves
1 garlic clove, peeled and mashed
3 tablespoons butter or margarine
½ cup olive oil

1. Place all ingredients except the olive oil and 2 tablespoons grated Asiago or Parmesan cheese in a food processor. (A blender works, too, but requires much stopping and going and scraping down the mixture.) As you purée or blend, slowly add the olive oil. Process or blend into a smooth paste.
2. Place blended pesto in a bowl. Reserve.

Chicken Scaloppine Marsala

Flour for dredging
Salt
4 boned chicken breasts, halved
2 eggs, beaten
Fine dried bread crumbs
3 tablespoons olive oil
3 tablespoons dry marsala (optional)

1. Spread the flour on 2 overlapping sheets of wax paper.
2. Lightly salt the breasts and dredge them in flour. Dip into the beaten eggs, then dredge in bread crumbs.
3. In a large frying pan over medium heat, heat the olive oil and evenly brown the chicken breasts, turning often. They should be thoroughly cooked and just golden brown in about 20 minutes. Add more oil, if necessary.
4. Remove chicken breasts. Pour the marsala into the frying pan, reduce heat, and deglaze the pan, stirring, for about 5 minutes.
5. Return the chicken breasts to the frying pan, moving them about in the sauce to coat them completely. Remove from heat and reserve, keeping them warm.
6. Place reserved beans in a pot over low heat.
7. Add 2 tablespoons of hot water to the reserved pesto in its bowl. Blend well. The water will somewhat lighten this powerful basil mixture.
8. Stir one-third of the pesto sauce into the beans in their pot, blending well but carefully. Do not add more pesto sauce; it will overpower the beans. Continue to heat the beans over low heat, stirring.
9. Place the reserved chicken breasts in their frying pan over medium heat, turning them once as they heat.
10. Serve a generous spoonful of the hot beans beside each serving of hot scaloppine on 4 individual warm plates. Lightly sprinkle

the reserved 2 tablespoons of Asiago or Parmesan cheese over the pesto-beans.

Note: Freeze remaining pesto sauce. It freezes very well.

Serves 4.

Cannellini Beans with Sole Palermo

We discovered this dish in a small seafood restaurant in Palermo. As so often happens in Sicily, seafood and various meats are interestingly paired with legumes, mainly beans.

Two 1-pound cans cannellini beans, drained, rinsed, and drained again
¼ cup extra virgin olive oil
2 tablespoons minced broad-leaf parsley
Salt and freshly ground black pepper to taste
4 garlic cloves, peeled and left whole
¼ cup freshly squeezed lemon juice
¾ cup dry white wine (optional)
4 sole fillets

1. Place drained beans in a bowl, add 2 tablespoons olive oil, the parsley, salt, and pepper, and toss well. You can heat the beans or serve them at room temperature.
2. Pour in the remaining 2 tablespoons olive oil into a baking dish and add the garlic, lemon juice, and white wine, blending well.
3. Arrange the sole fillets on top of the wine mixture, skin side down. Bake, uncovered, in a preheated 400 F oven for 10 minutes, or until the fish barely flakes when tested. They should not be overcooked.
4. Serve fish on individual plates along with a generous serving of beans.

Serves 4.

Chick-peas and Bulgur Wheat
with Lamb

    4 cups beef broth, homemade or canned
1½ pounds lean lamb, cubed
    2 cups dried chick-peas, soaked overnight covered with
       water, then drained
    2 tablespoons butter or margarine
1½ cups bulgur wheat
    2 cups plain low-fat yogurt

1. In a covered pot over medium heat, bring the beef broth to a boil. Reduce heat to low.
2. Add the lamb and chick-peas. Simmer, covered, 40 minutes, or until the chick-peas and lamb are tender.
3. In a saucepan over medium heat, melt the butter or margarine. Add the bulgur wheat and cook, stirring, for 5 minutes.
4. Stir the bulgur wheat and butter into the chick-peas and lamb. Simmer, stirring, for 5 minutes. Then simmer for 20 minutes more. Taste for seasoning, adding salt and pepper, if needed.
5. Spoon equal portions of this dish onto warm individual plates. Pass the yogurt at the table as an optional sauce or dressing for each serving.

Serves 4.

Chick-peas with Macaroni

3 tablespoons olive oil
1 large red onion, peeled and chopped
1 large sweet red pepper, cored, seeded, and chopped
One 14½-ounce can whole tomatoes, drained and chopped
Salt and freshly ground black pepper to taste
½ teaspoon dried basil
2 cups elbow macaroni
Two 15-ounce cans chick-peas, drained, rinsed, and
    drained again
¼ cup grated Asiago or Parmesan cheese

1. Over medium heat, heat the olive oil in saucepan and cook the onion and pepper for 10 minutes, stirring, until they are soft. Do not brown.
2. Stir in the chopped tomatoes, salt, pepper, and basil and cook over medium heat, stirring occasionally, for 15 minutes, or until the tomatoes have lost their watery consistency. Reserve.
3. In a pot over high heat, bring 2 quarts of water and 1½ teaspoons of salt to a boil. Stir in the macaroni, reduce heat to medium, and cook for 15 minutes, or until macaroni is just about soft, not mushy. Drain.
4. Place drained macaroni in pot in which it cooked. Stir in the reserved tomato mixture and the chick-peas.
5. Cook over medium heat, stirring, until hot, about 10 minutes.
6. Serve immediately in warm soup bowls, sprinkled with grated cheese.

Serves 4.

Garbanzo Salad with
Shrimp, Spanish Style

In Spain, this salad is sometimes served hot, sometimes cold. Try it each way.

Chick-pea Mixture

- 2 tablespoons olive oil
- 1 cup pea pods, washed and dried
- 1 small yellow sweet pepper, cored, seeded, and chopped
- 6 scallions, white part only, chopped
- Two 15-ounce cans chick-peas (garbanzos), drained, rinsed, and drained again
- 3 tablespoons freshly squeezed lemon juice
- ½ teaspoon salt
- ⅛ teaspoon dried red pepper flakes

1. In a saucepan over medium heat, heat the olive oil and cook the pea pods, yellow pepper, and scallions for 5 minutes, or until crisp-tender.
2. Blend in the chick-peas, lemon juice, salt, and red pepper flakes, mixing well.
3. Heat, stirring, for 5 minutes. Taste for seasoning, adding more salt and lemon juice, if desired.

Shrimp

- 1½ pounds medium-sized shrimp, shelled and deveined
- 1 cup dry Spanish sherry (optional)
- ¼ cup extra virgin olive oil
- 4 large garlic cloves, peeled and mashed
- Salt and freshly ground black pepper to taste
- 2 tablespoons minced fresh broad-leaf parsley

1. Place the shrimp, sherry, olive oil, and garlic in a bowl. Season with salt and pepper and blend well. Marinate in refrigerator for 3 hours.
2. Discard the garlic and place shrimp and marinade in a saucepan. Let sit for 1 hour for shrimp and marinade to reach room temperature.
3. Cook over high heat for 2 minutes, or just until the shrimp turn pink. Do not overcook or shrimp will become hard.
4. While shrimp are still heating, sprinkle them with parsley.
5. Serve the shrimp beside the hot chick-peas on warm plates, topping the shrimp with a large spoonful of their sauce. Garnish with toast strips for dunking in the shrimp sauce.

Serves 4.

Barbecued Salted Shrimp
and Chick-peas

This is an easy and innovative combination to serve outdoors in the summer. The chick-peas make a surprisingly different taste treat.

Chick-peas

Two 15-ounce cans chick-peas, drained, rinsed, and
    drained again
1½ teaspoons salt, or to taste
½ teaspoon dried tarragon
Juice of 2 limes, strained

1. Place chick-peas in a pot. Add the salt, tarragon, and lime juice and blend.
2. Set on back of the grill, stirring occasionally. They should be served hot. Taste for seasoning.

Shrimp

2 pounds jumbo shrimp, deveined and butterflied, but
    with shells left on
Salt
½ cup (1 stick) margarine
2 tablespoons freshly squeezed lemon juice

1. Thirty minutes before broiling, salt the fleshy part of the shrimp well.
2. Barbecue shrimp over glowing coals, flesh side down, for 2 minutes.
3. Turn and cook, shell side down, 4 minutes.
4. Melt the margarine in a pan over the coals. Pour in the lemon juice, blending well. Spoon hot mixture over shrimp on individual plates, accompanied by hot chick-peas.

Serves 4 generously.

Lamb with Fava Beans,
Roman Style

We found this dish in a tiny Roman trattoria. Not far from Rome, sheep and lambs graze in meadows and fields where wild rosemary grows in abundance, giving the flesh of the grazing animals an unusual and delicate flavor. In this recipe we try to duplicate that flavor by adding the rosemary. Use it carefully, as it is a strong herb that can easily overpower the other flavors.

Twenty 1-inch cubes lean fresh lamb, preferably cut from
    the leg
Salt and freshly ground black pepper
Flour for dredging
¼ cup olive oil
½ cup dry red wine (optional)
2 cups beef broth, homemade or canned
1 cup scraped, diced carrots
1 cup chopped onions
½ teaspoon dried rosemary
Two 15-ounce cans fava beans, drained and rinsed

1. Sprinkle the lamb lightly with salt and pepper. Spread flour on wax paper and dredge the lamb cubes well.
2. In an ovenproof casserole, heat the olive oil over medium heat and evenly brown the lamb. Pour the wine over the browned lamb and stir well, deglazing the pan.
3. Add the beef broth, carrots, onions, and rosemary, blending well.
4. Bring to a boil, cover the casserole, and place in a preheated 350 F oven for 45 minutes, or until the lamb is just tender. Taste for seasoning.
5. Stir in the fava beans and return to oven for 10 minutes to heat beans through (or heat on top of stove). Serve on warm plates.

Serves 4.

Green Beans with Scallops

1   tablespoon sherry vinegar
1½ pounds fresh young, tender green beans, trimmed
1   medium-sized onion, peeled and chopped
2   tablespoons extra virgin olive oil
2   garlic cloves, peeled and chopped
¾   pound bay scallops (or sea scallops cut in half)
Salt and freshly ground black pepper to taste

1. Half fill a saucepan with water and bring to a boil over high heat. Stir in the vinegar and green beans. Return to a boil and cook for 3 minutes.
2. Drain beans and plunge into fresh cold water. Drain. Dry beans with paper towels.
3. In a frying pan over medium heat, cook the onion and beans in the olive oil for 5 minutes.
4. Add the garlic and scallops, seasoning with salt and pepper, and simmer over low heat, stirring, for 10 minutes, or until the scallops and beans are just tender. Do not overcook.

Serves 4.

Kidney Beans and Ham
Casserole

Served over rice, this dish makes a satisfying lunch or light supper.

 2 tablespoons butter or margarine
 1 large onion, peeled and finely chopped
 2 cups diced cooked ham
 1 tablespoon flour
 ½ cup homemade Chicken Broth (page 13), or canned
 1 cup dry red wine (optional)
 ½ teaspoon salt
 Dash cayenne pepper
 Two 15-ounce cans red kidney beans, drained and rinsed
 4 strips bacon (optional)

1. In a large frying pan over medium-high heat, melt the butter or margarine and cook the onion until soft. Do not brown.
2. Stir in the ham, blending with the onion. Sprinkle in the flour, blending. Add the chicken broth and wine, stirring well. Add the salt and cayenne. Stir. Cook 10 minutes.
3. Add the kidney beans, blending well.
4. Place bean mixture in a casserole, top with the bacon strips, and cook in a preheated 350 F oven, uncovered, for 20 minutes, or until completely heated through and bacon is crisp.

Serves 2 to 4.

Mexican Kidney Beans with Ground Turkey

3 tablespoons extra virgin olive oil
1 large onion, peeled and chopped
1 pound ground turkey (available in most markets)
½ teaspoon salt
½ teaspoon chili powder
One 16-ounce can red kidney beans, drained, rinsed, and drained again
One 10-ounce can enchilada sauce (available in most markets)
1½ cups shredded sharp Cheddar cheese

1. In a large saucepan, heat the olive oil over medium heat and sauté the onion, stirring, for 5 minutes.
2. Stir in the ground turkey, seasoning with salt, and blend with the onions. Cook, stirring occasionally, for 15 minutes.
3. Stir in the chili powder, beans, and enchilada sauce, blending well. Reduce heat to low and cook, stirring, for 15 minutes. Taste for seasoning.
4. Sprinkle with the shredded cheese, cover pot, and keep on low heat until the cheese begins melting. Serve over rice.

Serves 4.

Legumed Chicken with
Celery Sauce in Pastry Shells

One 10¾-ounce can condensed cream of celery soup
    mixed with ½ can milk
2 tablespoons butter or margarine
1½ cups fresh green beans, trimmed and cut in strips
1½ cups snow peas, sliced diagonally into ½-inch pieces
¼ pound fresh small mushrooms, sliced
Salt and freshly ground black pepper to taste
2 cups diced cooked chicken
2 tablespoons dry marsala wine (optional)
One 10-ounce package commercial puff-pastry shells,
    baked according to package directions

1. In a saucepan large enough to hold all ingredients except puff
   pastry, heat the celery soup and milk, stirring, over medium
   heat. Reserve and keep warm.
2. In a frying pan over medium heat, melt the butter or margarine.
   Stir in the green beans, snow peas, and mushrooms, sprinkle
   with salt and pepper, and stir-fry until crisp-tender.
3. Stir the vegetables, cooked chicken, and marsala wine into the
   celery soup, blending well. Stir over medium heat until the vegetables and soup are hot, but do not boil. Taste for seasoning.
4. Spoon mixture into warm, baked pastry shells, and serve
   immediately.

Serves 6.

Double Legumes with Chicken Franks

    3 tablespoons olive oil
    1 medium-sized onion, peeled and finely chopped
    2 celery stalks, scraped and finely chopped
    1 small garlic clove, peeled and minced
 1½ pounds chicken franks, cut into slices slightly less than
       ½-inch thick
   ½ cup quartered pitted black olives
 One 6-ounce can tomato juice
    1 teaspoon Worcestershire sauce
 Salt and freshly ground black pepper to taste
 One 16-ounce can kidney beans, drained, rinsed, and
       drained again
 One 16-ounce can chick-peas, drained, rinsed, and
       drained again
    1 cup shredded Gouda or Cheddar cheese
    2 cups orzo (rice-shaped pasta), cooked in boiling salted
       water al dente and kept hot

1. In a saucepan, heat the olive oil over medium heat. Add the
   onion, celery, and garlic and sauté until soft, but do not brown.
2. Add the chicken franks and cook over medium heat until heated
   through.
3. Add the olives, tomato juice, Worcestershire sauce, salt, pepper,
   kidney beans, and chick-peas and simmer 5 minutes, until thoroughly heated. Add half the cheese and stir until melted. Taste
   for seasoning.
4. Add the remaining cheese to the hot orzo and stir until melted.
5. Serve the chicken frank mixture over the orzo.

Serves 6.

Lentils with Catfish Fillets

At our home recently we served farm-raised catfish, one of the tastiest and safest of fish, over savory lentils. Our guests were surprised and delighted—those tiny lentils with the big taste have a way of doing this.

¼ cup olive oil
1 large onion, peeled and finely chopped
1½ cups dried lentils, picked over, well rinsed, and drained
3 cups homemade Chicken Broth (page 13), or canned
4 catfish fillets (each weighing ½ pound)
¼ cup flour for dredging
3 eggs, beaten with 1 teaspoon of salt
5 tablespoons bread crumbs for dredging

1. In a pot, heat 1 tablespoon olive oil over medium heat. Stir in the onion and cook until soft. Do not brown.
2. Stir in the lentils, cover with the chicken broth, stir, cover the pot, and simmer for 40 minutes, stirring occasionally, until the lentils are just soft. Do not overcook. Lentils should be tender but not mushy. Taste for seasoning, adding salt, if needed. The broth may have supplied enough. Keep warm.
3. Pour the remaining 3 tablespoons olive oil into a frying pan just before preparing the catfish.
4. Spread the flour on wax paper. Lightly dredge the catfish in the flour.
5. Place the beaten eggs and salt in a large shallow bowl and beat lightly again. Dip the dredged catfish well in the beaten egg, covering both sides.
6. Spread the bread crumbs on wax paper and dredge the egg-dipped catfish in the crumbs.
7. Heat the frying pan with the olive oil over medium-high heat. Add the prepared catfish fillets and evenly brown on both sides.

8. With a slotted spoon, divide the warm lentils in equal amounts among 4 individual plates. Place 1 catfish fillet atop each mound of lentils. Serve immediately.

Serves 4.

Lentils and Potatoes with Chicken Sausages

2½ cups dried lentils
  2 large onions, peeled and coarsely chopped
  2 garlic cloves, peeled and finely chopped
  1 teaspoon dried basil
  3 medium-sized potatoes, peeled and quartered
  1 pound chicken sausages, parboiled 10 minutes, then
    cut into 1-inch pieces
   Salt to taste

1. Pick over the lentils, discarding any foreign material. Rinse and drain.
2. Put the lentils in a pot and add enough water to cover them by 1 inch. Add the onions, garlic, and basil. Cover and bring to a boil over medium heat. Reduce heat and simmer for 15 minutes.
3. Add the potatoes, sausages, and salt. Simmer, covered, until the vegetables and lentils are tender, about 20 minutes.

Serves 4 to 6.

Mung Beans with Shellfish

1½ cups mung beans
 2 tablespoons extra virgin olive oil
 2 large garlic cloves, peeled and chopped
 3 shallots, peeled and chopped
 ½ pound sea scallops, quartered
12 large fresh shrimp, shelled, deveined, and halved
    lengthwise
 ½ cup tomato juice cocktail
    Salt to taste

1. Pick over the beans, discarding any foreign material. Rinse and drain. Cover with water and soak for 1 hour. Drain.
2. In a saucepan over medium heat, bring the beans and 4 cups of water to a boil. Reduce heat and simmer 30 minutes, or until beans are tender. Drain the beans and keep them hot.
3. Over medium heat in a saucepan large enough to hold all ingredients, heat the olive oil. Add the garlic and shallots and cook, stirring, 5 minutes, or until soft. Do not brown.
4. Add the scallops and shrimp. Pour in the tomato juice cocktail and cook, covered, over medium heat for 10 minutes, or until the shrimp turn pink and the scallops are firm.
5. Add the hot mung beans, blending thoroughly. Taste for seasoning, then add salt, if necessary.

Serves 4.

Navy Bean Chowder

On a cold winter's day we often enjoy this hearty dish. It makes an uncomplicated and satisfying Saturday night supper.

1½ cups dried navy (pea) beans
1½ teaspoons salt, plus additional for final seasoning
2 medium-sized potatoes, peeled and diced
1 large onion, peeled and chopped
1 tablespoon flour blended with 1 tablespoon butter or margarine
1½ cups chopped canned tomatoes
1 large green pepper, cored, seeded, and chopped
2 cups milk
Freshly ground black pepper

1. Pick over beans, discarding any foreign objects; rinse and drain. Soak beans in water to cover overnight; or boil in water for 2 minutes, remove from heat, cover, and soak 1 to 2 hours. Drain.
2. Place beans in a deep pot. Add salt and enough water to just cover the beans. Cover pot, bring to a boil over high heat, reduce heat to low, and simmer 30 minutes, or until tender but not soft or mushy. Stir occasionally. If water cooks off before beans are tender, add a small amount of *hot* water.
3. Stir in the potatoes and onion and simmer for 20 minutes, or until the potatoes are tender but not soft or mushy.
4. Stir the flour-butter mixture into the bean-potato pot, blending.
5. Add the tomatoes and green pepper and simmer over low heat, stirring frequently for 10 minutes, or until the "chowder" has thickened. Blend in the milk. Taste for seasoning, adding salt and pepper as needed.

Serves 6.

Peas and Chicken Pilaf

This tasty, nutritious dish is reasonably easy to assemble. We usually use leftover roast chicken, or sometimes buy ready-cooked nuggets of chicken or turkey breast. We also vary the dish by using frozen baby limas.

      3 tablespoons olive oil
      2 large onions, peeled and coarsely chopped
   1½ cups long-grain converted rice
      3 cups homemade Chicken Broth (page 13), or canned
Two 10-ounce packages frozen green peas, defrosted just
          enough to break into chunks
   3½ cups coarsely chopped cooked chicken or turkey
         Salt and freshly ground black pepper to taste
      ⅛ teaspoon saffron

1. In a deep saucepan over medium heat, heat the olive oil and
   sauté the onions until soft. Do not brown.
2. Stir in rice, chicken broth, frozen chunks of peas, and chicken;
   sprinkle in salt, pepper, and saffron. Stir well to blend.
3. Cover pan, reduce heat, and simmer for 20 minutes, or until
   rice is cooked, peas are tender, and liquid is absorbed. Fluff
   pilaf with a fork, and serve very hot.

Serves 4.

Creamed Peas with Salmon Croquettes

Peas

Two 10-ounce packages frozen tiny peas

Cook the peas according to package directions. Drain.

Cream Sauce

2½ tablespoons butter or margarine
2½ tablespoons flour
1½ cups milk
½ teaspoon dried dill
Salt and freshly ground black pepper to taste

1. In a saucepan over medium heat, melt the butter or margarine.
2. Add the flour, stirring it into a smooth paste. Gradually pour in the milk, stirring constantly, until smooth and thickened. Add the dried dill, salt, and pepper. Taste for seasoning.
3. Stir the peas into the cream sauce. Reserve. Heat before serving.

Salmon Croquettes

One 1-pound can red salmon
2 tablespoons butter or margarine
4 shallots, peeled and finely chopped
2 small, tender celery stalks, scraped and finely chopped
2 small eggs, beaten
½ cup fine dry bread crumbs, plus additional for dredging
2 tablespoons cream

1 teaspoon salt
½ teaspoon freshly ground black pepper
2 tablespoons olive oil

1. Drain the salmon, saving the liquid. Remove and discard the skin and bones.
2. In a saucepan over medium heat, melt the butter or margarine and sauté the shallots and celery until soft. Do not brown.
3. In a bowl, combine and blend well with a fork the salmon, shallots, celery, eggs, ½ cup bread crumbs, cream, salt, and pepper. While blending, add just enough of the salmon liquid to make a somewhat soft mixture that can be shaped into 4 croquettes that firmly hold their shape.
4. Dredge the croquettes with additional bread crumbs.
5. In a frying pan over medium heat, heat the olive oil and evenly brown the croquettes.
6. Serve on individual plates atop generous portions of hot creamed peas.

Serves 4.

Syrian Lamb with Peas

This Middle Eastern dish is usually served with hot bulgur wheat.

 3 tablespoons butter or margarine
 2 tablespoons olive oil
 3 pounds lean lamb from the leg, cut into 1½-inch cubes
Salt and freshly ground black pepper
 2 garlic cloves, peeled and minced
 3 tablespoons flour
 2 cups homemade Chicken Broth (page 13), or canned
 ½ cup tomato purée
18 small white onions, peeled and root ends scored
 ½ teaspoon cinnamon
 2 cups hulled fresh peas, slightly undercooked in boiling
    salted water, or one 10-ounce package frozen peas,
    defrosted but not cooked

1. In a deep pot, heat the butter and oil over medium heat. Sprinkle the lamb with salt and pepper and brown evenly.
2. Add the garlic and cook 1 minute.
3. Pour off any fat remaining in the pot. Sprinkle the lamb with flour, shaking the pot to distribute it. Stir in the broth, small amounts at a time, until all has been used; then blend in the tomato purée.
4. Add the onions and cinnamon and stir. Cover the pot and simmer over low heat for 45 minutes, or until the lamb and onions are fork-tender, shaking the pot from time to time so contents won't stick. If the sauce is too thick, add a small amount of hot broth.
5. Stir in the peas and simmer, covered, 10 minutes. Taste for seasoning.

Serves 6.

Pinto Bean Casserole
with Pork Chops

2 cups dried pinto or pink beans
Four 1-inch-thick smoked pork chops, bones removed, cut
   the long way in medium-thick slices
2 cups sauerkraut, well drained
1½ cups tomato purée
2 tablespoons olive oil
2 medium-sized onions, peeled and chopped
1½ tablespoons flour

1. Cover the beans with water and soak 5 hours; or boil in water 2
   minutes, remove from heat, cover, and soak for 1 to 2 hours.
   Drain.
2. Place beans and pork in a large pot and cover with water. Bring
   to a boil over high heat, then skim and reduce heat to low.
3. Cover the pot and simmer for 1½ hours, or until beans are just
   tender.
4. In another small pot, place sauerkraut and tomato purée, blending well. Cook over medium heat, uncovered, stirring frequently, for 10 minutes.
5. In a saucepan over medium heat, heat the olive oil and sauté the
   onions for 5 minutes. Do not brown. Sprinkle the flour into the
   onions and oil, and cook, stirring, until mixture is slightly thickened and golden.
6. Spoon cooked beans and pork slices into a casserole. Stir in the
   sauerkraut–tomato purée mixture and the floured onions,
   blending well.
7. Cover the casserole and place in a preheated 350 F oven for 20
   minutes, or until bean mixture is bubbling.

Serves 4.

Pinto Beans with Turkey Sausage

Italian-style turkey sausage, available in most supermarkets, is a delicious low-calorie, low-fat treat. We sometimes serve noodles with this dish, along with 2 pieces of sausage per serving. But noodles aren't essential; the beans and sausages are enough to make a satisfying meal.

1½ pounds Italian-style turkey sausage, cut into 8 equal pieces
¼ cup extra virgin olive oil
2 large onions, peeled and chopped
1 cup tomato sauce
½ teaspoon sugar
1 cup dry white wine (optional)
1 teaspoon salt
1 teaspoon dried oregano
One 2-pound can or two 16-ounce cans pinto beans, drained, rinsed, then drained again
1 cup homemade Chicken Broth (page 13), or canned

1. Prick the sausages in several places. Place them in a saucepan, cover with water, and bring to a boil over high heat. Reduce heat to low and simmer for 10 minutes. Remove and dry sausages with paper towels. Discard liquid.
2. In a large frying pan, place olive oil, sausages, and onions, and cook over low heat, stirring onions and turning sausages, for 10 minutes.
3. Stir in the tomato sauce, sugar, wine, salt, and oregano. Bring to a boil over high heat. Reduce heat to low and simmer, uncovered, stirring, for 7 minutes.
4. Place pinto beans and chicken stock in a large pot. Stir in the contents of the frying pan, blending well with the beans. Loosely cover pot and simmer over low heat for 25 minutes.

Serves 4.

Pink Beans with
Chicken Thighs

 2 cups dried pink beans
1½ teaspoons salt
 2 garlic cloves, peeled and left whole
 2 small bay leaves
 2 tablespoons extra virgin olive oil
 ¼ cup minced salt pork (optional)
 2 medium-sized onions, peeled and chopped
 6 large chicken thighs
Salt and freshly ground black pepper to taste
 ¼ teaspoon dried rosemary
 ½ teaspoon dry mustard
Chicken Broth (optional; page 13)

1. Soak the beans overnight in water to cover; or boil in water 2 minutes, remove from heat, cover, and soak 1 to 2 hours. Drain.
2. Place beans, salt, garlic, and bay leaves in a large pot. Cover with boiling water and simmer, covered, for 1½ hours, or until the beans are tender but not mushy. Drain beans and reserve all of the cooking liquid. Discard garlic and bay leaves.
3. Heat the olive oil in a large frying pan over medium heat. Add the salt pork and cook until its fat is rendered. Stir in the onions and sauté 5 minutes, or until soft. Do not brown.
4. With a slotted spoon transfer the salt pork and onions to a casserole. Set aside.
5. Sear chicken thighs evenly in frying pan with olive oil and rendered salt pork fat, seasoning lightly with salt and pepper. Transfer thighs to waiting casserole with salt pork and onions.
6. Blend in the beans, rosemary, and dry mustard. Pour in the reserved bean cooking liquid to cover all ingredients. If there is not enough liquid to cover, add chicken broth. Place in a preheated 350 F oven, covered, for 2 hours, or until beans and chicken are tender. Check the casserole periodically. If liquid cooks off too quickly before beans and chicken are tender, add *hot* chicken broth. Taste for seasoning.

Serves 6.

Snow Peas, Bean Sprouts, and Chicken Breasts, Chinese Style

5 tablespoons light (low-sodium) soy sauce
2 teaspoons sugar
2 tablespoons dry white wine (optional)
2 tablespoons cornstarch
2 whole boned chicken breasts, cut into large dice
2 tablespoons peanut oil
1 cup snow peas
1 cup bean sprouts
½ cup bamboo shoots, shredded
3 tablespoons dry sherry (optional)

1. In a large bowl, combine 3 tablespoons soy sauce, 1 teaspoon sugar, the white wine, and cornstarch. Blend well. Add the chicken and coat it well with this mixture. Marinate the chicken for 2 hours in refrigerator, stirring occasionally. Drain off any excess liquid.
2. Over medium-high heat, heat the peanut oil in a frying pan or wok, and stir-fry the diced chicken for 4 minutes.
3. Stir in the snow peas, bean sprouts, bamboo shoots, the remaining 2 tablespoons soy sauce, the remaining 1 teaspoon sugar, and the sherry.
4. Stir-fry for 3 minutes, or until the chicken is fork-tender but the vegetables are still crisp. Serve with liberal portions of plain boiled rice.

Serves 4.

Sole Strips with Snow Peas

6 sole fillets
¼ cup flour
2 eggs, beaten
Salt and freshly ground black pepper to taste
½ cup peanut oil
1 cup sliced fresh mushrooms
1 pound snow peas
½ cup chopped peeled shallots
2 tablespoons light (low-sodium) soy sauce
1 teaspoon sugar
2 tablespoons homemade Chicken Broth (page 13), or canned
2 teaspoons cornstarch
½ cup toasted almond slivers

1. Cut the fish fillets into narrow (about 1½-inch) strips.
2. In a bowl, blend the flour, eggs, salt, and pepper.
3. Over medium heat, heat the oil in a frying pan. Dip the fish in the egg-flour mixture, and fry in oil until golden, turning to evenly color the strips. Remove and keep warm.
4. If the oil has been absorbed by the fish, add a small amount of additional peanut oil and sauté the mushrooms for 5 minutes. Add the snow peas and shallots and cook 5 minutes, stirring constantly.
5. Combine the soy sauce, sugar, chicken broth, and cornstarch, and add the mixture to the pan, blending well. Cook over low heat for 5 minutes, stirring.
6. Arrange the fish strips on top of the vegetables and sprinkle with the almond slivers.

Serves 6.

Split Pea and Chicken Combination Casserole

½ pound dried yellow split peas
½ pound dried green split peas
2 garlic cloves, peeled and crushed
1½ teaspoons salt
2 tablespoons butter or margarine
1 large onion, peeled and chopped
2 tablespoons olive oil
4 medium-sized chicken legs
4 medium-sized chicken thighs
½ teaspoon dried thyme
¼ teaspoon dried rosemary
One 10-ounce can condensed cream of mushroom soup
⅔ cup milk

1. Pick over the peas, discarding any foreign material and imperfect peas.
2. In a pot, bring 5 cups of water to a boil over high heat. Stir in the split peas. Return to a boil, add the garlic, and boil 2 minutes. Stir in the salt. Cover and let stand off heat 30 minutes. Remove and discard the garlic.
3. In a large saucepan over medium heat, melt the butter or margarine. Add the onion and sauté 5 minutes, or until soft. Do not brown. With a slotted spoon, transfer the onion to a small bowl and reserve.
4. Add the olive oil to the saucepan, and brown the chicken evenly over medium heat, adding more oil if needed.
5. Drain the peas and spoon them evenly into a casserole. Spread the reserved onion over the peas.
6. Arrange the browned chicken over peas and onion. Evenly sprinkle the herbs over all.
7. Pour the mushroom soup and milk into the pan in which the chicken browned and, over medium heat, stir until smooth. Pour this sauce over the chicken in the casserole.

8. Cover the casserole and bake in a preheated 350 F oven for 1 hour, or until the chicken is tender. Remove cover for the last 10 minutes of cooking.

Serves 4.

White Kidney and Fava Beans
with Braised Lamb Shanks

We first had this savory dish in a bistro in Paris, and it's been a favorite ever since.

Beans

1½ cups dried white kidney beans
1½ cups dried fava beans

1. Soak the beans, covered with water, overnight, then drain. Peel off the bitter brown skins of the fava beans.
2. Place beans in a large pot, cover with water (three parts water to one part beans). Bring to a boil over high heat. Cover pot, reduce heat to low, and simmer for 2 hours, or until the beans are tender. Drain any liquid remaining in the bean pot. Reserve the beans.

Lamb Shanks

About 3 tablespoons olive oil
6 lamb shanks
Salt and freshly ground black pepper to taste
2 cups beef broth, homemade or canned
2 large carrots, scraped and coarsely chopped
2 medium-sized onions, peeled and coarsely chopped
2 celery stalks (with leaves), scraped and coarsely chopped
2 bay leaves
About ⅛ teaspoon dried thyme
About ⅛ teaspoon dried rosemary
2 garlic cloves, peeled and minced
1 cup dry white wine (optional)

1. In a large frying pan over medium heat, heat the olive oil and brown lamb shanks evenly (add more oil, if needed). Sprinkle with salt and pepper.
2. Remove the lamb shanks and deglaze pan with the beef broth. Set aside.
3. Cover the bottom of a large, deep, ovenproof pot with the carrots, onions, and celery. Add the bay leaves and lightly sprinkle on thyme, rosemary, and garlic.
4. Arrange the lamb shanks on top. Add the beef broth and the white wine (or more broth). The vegetables should be barely covered.
5. Cover the pot, bring to a boil on top of the stove, then place in a preheated 300 F oven to bake for 3 hours, or until the lamb shanks are very tender. Discard bay leaves.
6. Remove the lamb shanks from the braising pot and stir the reserved beans into the liquid and vegetables. Place the pot over medium heat on top of the stove, stirring until the beans are hot.
7. Serve the lamb shanks on individual plates atop generous servings of beans.

Serves 6.

White Kidney Beans
and Halibut

Beans

Two 16-ounce cans white kidney beans (cannellini),
    drained, rinsed, and drained again
1 large red onion, peeled and finely chopped
1 large red pepper, cored, seeded, and finely chopped
1 teaspoon ground cumin
1 teaspoon ground coriander
3 tablespoons extra virgin olive oil
2 tablespoons balsamic vinegar
Salt and freshly ground black pepper to taste (optional)

1. Place beans in a large, deep saucepan.
2. Add the onion, red pepper, cumin, coriander, olive oil, and vinegar. Mix thoroughly but gently.
3. Taste for seasoning; salt and pepper may not be needed.
4. Heat the beans before serving.

Halibut

Six ½-pound halibut steaks
2 lemons, quartered, for garnish

1. Wash and dry fish.
2. Broil or grill thick, solid fish steaks such as halibut for 15 minutes, turning them to grill on the other side at the halfway point, after 7½ minutes. When properly cooked, fish will flake easily with a fork.
3. Spoon a substantial base of hot beans on individual warm plates, and top each serving of beans with a hot grilled halibut steak.
4. Garnish with lemon quarters.

Serves 6.

White Bean–Tomato Sauce
with Pork Hocks

Here's a unique version of the old favorite pork and beans. The beans act as a thickener when combined with the tomatoes on braised meat. Serve with rice or noodles.

¼ cup olive oil
6 meaty pork hocks or lean chops
2 garlic cloves, peeled and chopped
2 celery stalks, scraped and chopped
2 medium-sized carrots, scraped and chopped
2 medium-sized onions, peeled and chopped
1 teaspoon salt
½ teaspoon freshly ground black pepper
1 teaspoon dried thyme
One 28-ounce can whole tomatoes, drained and chopped
2 cups homemade Chicken Broth (page 13), or canned
1 cup white wine (optional)
Two 16-ounce cans white kidney beans, drained, rinsed,
    and drained again

1. In a large ovenproof pot over medium heat, heat the olive oil. Evenly brown the pork hocks or chops. Remove and reserve.
2. Add the garlic, celery, carrots, and onions to the pot. Sprinkle with salt and pepper. (If oil has been absorbed by the meat, add a small amount to the pot.) Cook over medium heat for 5 minutes, stirring.
3. Return the pork hocks to the pot. Add the thyme, tomatoes, broth, and wine. Bring to a boil over high heat. Cover pot and place in a preheated 300 F oven for 2 hours. Add the beans, return pot to the oven, and cook another 1 hour, or until the hocks are tender.
4. Remove the hocks. Place the bean-tomato mixture (reserve one-quarter of the beans to spoon over the pork hocks) in a food processor, processing into a medium-thick sauce.

5. Return the hocks to the pot. Add the processed bean-tomato sauce, then the reserved whole beans.
6. Cover and heat on top of the stove over medium-low heat.
7. Serve hot with the sauce spooned over the pork hocks and the whole beans spooned over the sauce.

Serves 6.

Black Bean Gumbo

This is a Creole dish, which means that both the Indians and the French had a hand in it; the native Louisianians also lent their own creative touch.

Black Beans, Peas, and Rice

1½ cups long-grain converted rice
2½ cups homemade Chicken Broth (page 13), or canned
One 16-ounce can black beans (frijoles negros), drained and rinsed
One 10-ounce package frozen peas, blanched in boiling water 3 minutes and drained

1. In a deep saucepan, combine the rice and the chicken broth, blending with a fork. Bring to a boil over medium-high heat. Reduce heat to low, cover pot, and simmer for 20 minutes, until the rice is just tender. If liquid cooks off before the rice is tender, add a little more hot broth. If the rice is cooked before the liquid is absorbed, uncover, raise heat and cook off liquid.
2. Stir in the black beans and peas, blending well with the rice. Reserve.

Gumbo

¼ cup bacon fat, or ½ stick butter or margarine
One 4-pound chicken, cut up
2 quarts water
One 1-pound can tomatoes, chopped (save the liquid)
⅛ teaspoon dried thyme
½ teaspoon cayenne, or to taste
⅛ teaspoon dried red pepper flakes, or to taste
1 teaspoon salt
1 large onion, peeled and chopped

1 large garlic clove, peeled and chopped
1 small sweet green pepper, cored, seeded, and chopped
1 small sweet red pepper, cored, seeded, and chopped
1 cup fresh okra, trimmed and cut into ½-inch slices
1 pint small fresh oysters
18 medium shrimp (about ½ pound), shelled and deveined
½ teaspoon hot sauce, or to taste

1. In a large pot, heat half the bacon fat, butter, or margarine, and evenly brown the chicken pieces over medium-high heat. Leave chicken in pot.
2. Add the water, tomatoes, thyme, cayenne, red pepper flakes, and salt. Simmer over medium heat, covered, 35 minutes, or until the chicken is tender.
3. Take the chicken from liquid and remove meat from the bones. Reserve liquid and chicken meat separately. Discard bones.
4. Simmer the liquid in the pot, until reduced to about 1½ quarts. Strain and set aside.
5. In the pot, heat the remaining bacon fat, butter, or margarine over medium-high heat. Sauté the onion, garlic, and sweet pepper until soft. Do not brown.
6. Pour the strained liquid into the pot, add the okra, and simmer 5 minutes. Add the oysters and shrimp and cook 5 minutes, or until the edges of the oysters curl, and the shrimp have just turned pink and are firm.
7. Stir in the chicken meat and hot sauce, blending all well.
8. Reheat the black beans, peas, and rice. Spoon them generously into 6 large hot individual rimmed soup bowls. Top with big spoonfuls of the gumbo.

Serves 6.

Boston Baked Beans

Although this dish was made famous in Boston, it soon became a national classic, with cooks in various parts of the country adding their own touches. Our mother and mother-in-law, Maria Cifelli Limoncelli, was famous for her "Boston" baked beans in her home town of Elmira, New York. She was frequently asked to bake them for church suppers and various school events. She didn't like the smaller navy beans that the Bostonians used, preferring the larger, lustier Great Northern beans. She also disapproved of taking shortcuts on this dish and always soaked the beans overnight. The salt pork is an essential part of the classic baked bean recipe.

>2 pounds dried Great Northern beans
>1 pound salt pork
>1 tablespoon salt
>1 cup molasses
>3 tablespoons sugar

1. Carefully pick over the beans, discarding any imperfect beans and foreign material. Cover with cold water and soak overnight. Drain well.
2. Place the beans in a large pot, cover with fresh water, and, over low heat, cook the beans, covered, maintaining the water just below boiling; 2 hours should do it.
3. To test, place a few beans on a tablespoon and blow on them. If properly cooked, the skins on the beans will burst and drop off. At this point drain the beans.
4. In a small pot, cover the salt pork with water, bring to a boil, and scald for 3 minutes. Drain and rinse well in cold water.
5. Cut enough ¼-inch-thick slices from the pork to line the bottom of a large ovenproof pot. Add the beans. In the remaining rind of the pork cut incisions about every ½ inch, the cuts 1 inch deep. Bury the pork rind in the beans in the pot.
6. In a bowl blend the salt, molasses, and sugar well. Stir in 1 cup boiling water and blend again. Pour the mixture over the beans.

7. Add just enough boiling water to cover the beans. Cover the pot and bake in a preheated 250 F oven for 6 hours. Remove the cover and bake for 1 hour more.

Serves 6.

Cassoulet à la Paysanne

This bean, duck, and sausage casserole is probably the most famous of the legume classics. It's also a signature dish of our mentor, Master Chef Antoine Gilly. There are several variations of cassoulet, which originated around Toulouse in southwestern France. The original version calls for preserved goose, which is not readily available in the states, so Antoine Gilly has substituted duck.

Beans

1 pound dried white marrow or Great Northern beans
6 cups clear homemade Chicken Broth (page 13), or canned
1 cup dry white wine
1 large onion, peeled and stuck with 2 cloves
1 large carrot, scraped and cut up
Bouquet garni (1 bay leaf, 2 sprigs parsley, 6 black peppercorns, ½ teaspoon dried thyme, tied in cheesecloth)
1 large garlic clove, peeled
2 teaspoons salt

1. Pick over the beans, discarding any discolored or imperfect ones and any foreign material. Rinse them and soak in cold, fresh water for 5 hours.
2. Drain the beans; place in a deep pot with the chicken broth, wine, onion, carrot, bouquet garni, garlic, and salt.
3. Cover and bring to a boil over high heat. Then place in a preheated 350 F oven for 30 minutes, or until the beans are slightly undercooked—still firm, but not hard.

Meats

One 4-pound duckling
Salt and freshly ground black pepper to taste

One 1-pound garlic sausage (Italian cotechino, or a French
  garlic sausage)
½ pound salt pork
2 pounds (boned) lean pork shoulder or loin
1 pound (boned) lean shoulder of lamb
2 large onions, peeled and chopped
1 cup tomato purée
1 cup dry white wine (optional)
1 cup homemade Chicken Broth (page 13), or canned
1 cup water
Bouquet garni (as listed above)
1 teaspoon salt
½ teaspoon freshly ground black pepper
1 cup dry bread crumbs
2 tablespoons butter or margarine

1. Sprinkle the duckling with salt and pepper. Place in a roasting
   pan and roast, uncovered, in a preheated 450 F oven for 1 hour,
   or until tender. Cool, then remove meat from the bones. Set
   aside. Reserve drippings in roasting pan.
2. Pierce the garlic sausage in several places and place it and the
   salt pork in a pot. Cover with water and simmer, covered, over
   medium heat for 1½ hours. Drain and discard liquid.
3. In a large pot over medium-high heat, heat the reserved duck
   drippings and brown the pork and the lamb, 1 piece at a time.
   Remove and set aside. In the same pot cook the chopped onions
   until soft. Do not brown. Stir in the tomato purée, wine, chicken
   broth, water, and bouquet garni. Add the browned pork and
   lamb, salt, and pepper. Simmer, covered, over medium heat for
   1½ hours, or until the meats are tender. Remove the pork and
   lamb; strain and reserve the cooking liquid.
4. Cut the duckling meat into bite-sized pieces and the salt pork
   into thin slices. Remove the skin from the sausage and cut into
   slices ¼ to ½ inch thick. Cut the pork and lamb into medium-
   thick slices.
5. Drain the cooked beans, but reserve the liquid. Strain the liquid,
   discarding the vegetables and the bouquet garni, and blend it
   with the cooking liquid from the pork and lamb.

6. Line the bottom of a deep large casserole with the slices of salt pork. Spoon in a layer of beans, then a layer of meat, sausage, or duckling. Continue alternating beans and meat, ending with beans.

7. Heat the reserved bean-and-meat liquid, and spoon in just enough to barely come to the top; do not cover the top layer of beans.

8. Sprinkle the top layer with bread crumbs and dot with butter. Place, uncovered, in a preheated 350 F oven for 45 minutes, or until the top layer is crusty and brown. Serve right from the casserole.

Serves 8.

Chick-peas and Honey
with Kibbeh

This dish originated in Beirut. The chick-peas are served with a ground lamb dish, kibbeh, a sort of Middle Eastern meat loaf, which is flavored with cracked wheat, pine nuts, onion, and tomato. The combination is memorable.

Chick-peas

2   cups dried chick-peas, soaked 8 hours and drained
2   tablespoons butter or margarine
1   tablespoon extra virgin olive oil
1   teaspoon salt
½   teaspoon freshly ground black pepper
¼   teaspoon cinnamon
½   cup honey

1. In a covered pot simmer the chick-peas, covered with water (3 parts water to 1 part peas), for 1½ hours, or until just tender. Drain and transfer to a casserole.
2. Add the butter or margarine, olive oil, salt, pepper, cinnamon, and honey and blend well. Taste for seasoning. Shortly before serving, bake, uncovered, in a preheated 350 F oven for 20 minutes, or until completely heated through.

Kibbeh

½   cup bulgur (cracked wheat)
½   cup hot homemade Chicken Broth (page 13), or canned
1½ pounds lamb, ground twice (use lean portions of shoulder, or shanks)
1   medium-sized onion, peeled and minced
1   cup tomato sauce
1   teaspoon salt

½ teaspoon freshly ground black pepper
½ teaspoon ground cumin
½ cup pine nuts
¼ cup melted butter

1. In a large bowl, mix the bulgur with the chicken stock and let stand 2 hours. The stock should be completely absorbed.
2. Combine the lamb, onion, tomato sauce, salt, pepper, and cumin with the bulgur in its bowl, blending well.
3. Butter or oil a shallow 9-by-10-inch pan, and evenly spread the meat mixture in it.
4. Push the pine nuts into the flat meat cake, studding the entire cake. Pour on the melted butter. Place on the center rack position in a preheated 375 F oven and bake for 25 mintues, or until crusty on top.
5. Slice and serve hot with the hot chick-peas.

Serves 6.

Cocido

We have in our possession several unique handmade Spanish wooden spoons, ranging from one that is ornately carved, its bowl twice as large as an open hand, to one that is the size of an ordinary serving spoon, delicately scrolled and carved. The larger one is used to dip into the cocido pot—it then serves as a plate for the smaller spoon. This is the system used by Spanish farmers who eat their midday meal while working in the fields.

Any variety of legumes, meats, and fowl can be used in this classic Spanish boiled dinner, but inexpensive cuts of beef, ham, sausages, and chicken are the most popular. This is an exciting company dish that keeps well, so we suggest you make enough for several meals.

2 pounds beef bones
One 3-pound brisket of beef
6 quarts water
1 tablespoon salt
1 teaspoon freshly ground black pepper
1½ pounds lean smoked ham
½ pound fatback of pork, not salted (labeled in markets "pork for cooking beans") (optional)
8 chorizos (Spanish sausages), or any highly seasoned smoked pork sausage, blanched in boiling water 5 minutes
One 3-pound chicken, cut up
4 leeks, white part and some of the light green part, thoroughly cleaned and cut into halves lengthwise
8 small carrots, scraped
2 garlic cloves, peeled and left whole
1 large cabbage, trimmed and cored, cut into wedges
8 small potatoes, peeled
1 cup fine noodles
One 16-ounce can black beans (frijoles negros) drained, rinsed, drained again, and reserved

One 16-ounce can chick-peas drained, rinsed, drained
again, and reserved
2 tablespoons chopped fresh parsley

1. In a large deep pot, place the beef bones, beef brisket, water,
   salt, and pepper. Over high heat, bring to a boil; reduce heat to
   low and simmer, partially covered, for 1 hour, skimming any
   scum from the surface.
2. Add the ham, fatback, and sausages; simmer 30 minutes.
3. Add the chicken and simmer for 30 minutes; then add the leeks,
   carrots, garlic, cabbage, and potatoes. Simmer, partially covered, for 30 minutes, or until meats and vegetables are fork-
   tender. (If the chicken and vegetables are tender before the
   meat, remove them. Return them to the pot just before serving.)
4. Stir in the chick-peas and the black beans and simmer, uncovered, for 10 minutes. Check seasoning, adding salt and pepper,
   if needed. Remove and slice into serving portions the beef brisket, smoked ham, fatback of pork, and return them and the
   chicken to the pot.
5. While chick-peas and meats are heating, cook noodles al dente
   in boiling salted water; drain.
6. Just before serving, strain the entire contents of the pot through
   a large colander.
7. Serve the broth as a first course with the noodles and a sprinkling of black beans, chick-peas, and parsley. Next, as the main
   course, present the sliced meats, whole sausages, and chicken in
   a large serving dish, surrounded by the vegetables and legumes.

Serves 8.

Flageolets and Roast Leg
of Lamb

Flageolets, or baby kidney beans, look like immature limas. Taken from their pods when very young, they are a lovely pale green, also tender, somewhat mealy, but with a delicate flavor.

The French usually serve them with roast lamb *(gigot),* which has become a classic combination. In fact, we have seldom encountered them except in this twosome. They are quite difficult to find fresh, except occasionally in specialty and gourmet shops, but they are available both canned and dried. Use the canned variety for this recipe.

Flageolets

Two 15-ounce cans flageolets
2 tablespoons extra virgin olive oil
3 shallots, peeled and finely chopped
Salt and freshly ground black pepper to taste

1. Drain the flageolets, rinse well in fresh cold water, and drain again.
2. In a saucepan over medium heat, heat the olive oil and cook the shallots until soft. Do not brown.
3. Stir in the flageolets, season with salt and pepper, and blend well with the oil and shallots.

Roast Leg of Lamb

The French, masters of lamb cookery, handle that tender, tasty meat simply. This recipe for *gigot* is the perfect illustration. French cooks cook the lamb uncovered in a very hot oven at 15 minutes a pound and serve it rare, or quite pink. We are in complete agreement.

One 4-pound leg of lamb
1 large garlic clove, peeled and cut into 4 slivers
1 tablespoon olive oil
Salt and freshly ground black pepper

1. With a sharp knife make 4 well-spaced slits in the lamb leg and insert the garlic slivers.
2. Rub lightly with the olive oil, and season well with salt and pepper.
3. Place lamb in a roasting pan and roast, uncovered, in a preheated 450 F oven for 1 hour.
4. Remove lamb from oven and baste well with the pan juices. Cut into medium-thick slices, and serve with generous portions of hot flageolets.

Serves 6.

Frijoles Refritos
(Refried Beans)

We often make this classic Mexican dish to accompany chicken or fish.

3 tablespoons bacon drippings or vegetable oil
1 medium-sized onion, peeled and chopped
1 tablespoon flour
3 cups cooked pinto beans, well drained
¼ cup cooked tomato or tomato sauce
1 teaspoon salt
¼ teaspoon freshly ground black pepper
1 teaspoon chili powder

1. In a frying pan over medium heat, heat the bacon drippings or oil. Add the onion and cook until soft. Do not brown. Stir in the flour and cook, stirring, until golden.
2. Reduce heat to low and add the beans, 3 or 4 tablespoons at a time, and mash them with a fork. When all of the beans have been added and mashed, simmer 5 to 10 minutes, until all the fat is absorbed, stirring constantly to prevent burning.
3. Add the tomato or tomato sauce, salt, pepper, and chili powder. Blend well. Taste for seasoning. The bean mixture should be quite dry. If it seems too dry, add a small amount of chicken broth or more tomato sauce.

Serves 4.

Hopping John

This is a minor classic in the deep South. It's usually served on New Year's Day and, if eaten before noon, is said to bring good luck. In Georgia, home of the Vidalia onion, this dish is often accompanied by sliced sweet onion. You can vary the meat, substituting ham hocks or smoked boneless pork butt.

1½ cups dried black-eyed peas
One-pound piece lean bacon
1 onion, peeled and chopped
⅛ teaspoon dried red pepper flakes (optional)
6 cups water
1½ cups uncooked rice
1 teaspoon salt
Chopped fresh parsley for garnish
1 large Vidalia onion or red onion, thinly sliced

1. Pick over peas, discarding any foreign material and imperfect peas, and rinse thoroughly.
2. In a saucepan, combine the bacon, chopped onion, red pepper flakes, and water. Bring to a boil over high heat, reduce heat, cover, and simmer for 45 minutes.
3. With the water still simmering, gradually add the peas to the pan. Simmer, covered, for 45 minutes, or until the peas are almost tender. Stir occasionally.
4. Add the rice and salt and simmer 30 minutes, covered, or until the peas are tender and the rice is tender and fluffy. During the cooking, add more *hot* water if needed just to keep mixture moist. If there is too much liquid, remove cover and cook off the excess. Watch carefully, stirring occasionally to prevent burning.
5. Taste for seasoning, adding more salt, if needed.
6. Remove the bacon and cut it into thin slices.
7. Serve garnished with parsley, slices of bacon and sweet onion.

Serves 6.

Lentils and Cotechino Sausages

This remarkably flavorful lentil dish is a favorite in several European countries, and is combined with a variety of sausages. We discovered this particular version in Bologna.

1 pound dried lentils
Three 1-pound cotechino sausages
1 carrot, scraped and chopped
1 large celery stalk, scraped and chopped
2 garlic cloves, peeled and minced
¼ teaspoon dried thyme
2 medium-sized onions, peeled and chopped
5 tablespoons extra virgin olive oil
Salt and freshly ground black pepper to taste
About 3 cups homemade Chicken Broth (page 13), or canned
1 large fresh ripe tomato, peeled, seeded, and chopped
2 tablespoons chopped fresh parsley
1 teaspoon Hungarian paprika

1. Pick over lentils, discarding any foreign material, and rinse.
2. Prick the sausages in several places with the sharp point of a knife; place them in a deep pot, cover with water, bring to a boil over medium-high heat, reduce heat, cover, and simmer for 2 hours. Let sausages cool in the liquid.
3. Place the lentils in a deep pot and stir in the carrot, celery, minced garlic, thyme, half the chopped onions, 2 tablespoons olive oil, salt, pepper, and enough chicken broth to cover. Bring to a boil over medium-high heat. Reduce heat, cover, and simmer for 20 minutes.
4. Stir in the chopped tomato and continue to simmer, uncovered, until the lentils are tender but not mushy.
5. Drain the sausage; remove the skin and cut into ½-inch slices. Add them to the lentil pot.
6. In a frying pan over medium heat, heat the remaining 3 table-

spoons oil; cook the remaining onions and the parsley until the onions are soft. Do not brown. Stir in the paprika, and then blend this mixture into the lentil pot. Taste for seasoning. Simmer, uncovered, for 10 minutes.

7. Serve in warm rimmed soup dishes, with slices of crusty Italian bread.

Serves 6 to 8.

Paella

This celebrated national dish of Spain comes in several versions—with fish or game, sausage or shellfish, chicken or pork. But the most classic paella is the one we learned from the chef at Botin, probably Madrid's oldest and most popular restaurant.

Looking at the list of ingredients, it appears that paella is a complicated and time-consuming dish to make. Not really. Most of the main ingredients are cooked separately, then quickly assembled and simmered with the rice before serving.

The large circular paella pan, the *paellera,* is perfect for both cooking and serving this dish. If you cannot find one, use a very large, shallow (but not *too* shallow) pan that can go from the top of the stove into the oven.

½ cup extra virgin olive oil
One 3-pound chicken, cut up, breast cut into 4 pieces,
    thighs into 2 pieces each (do not use back or wing tips)
Salt and freshly ground black pepper to taste
8 pieces fresh haddock, each large enough for a small
    serving
1 large onion, peeled and chopped
2 garlic cloves, peeled and minced
1 cup raw lean pork, diced
1 large fresh tomato (or 1 cup canned), peeled, seeded,
    and chopped
3 cups converted long-grain rice
½ teaspoon powdered saffron
6 cups homemade Chicken Broth (page 13), or canned
1 cup fresh green peas, undercooked in salted water, or
    defrosted frozen peas
One 16-ounce can chick-peas, rinsed and drained
1 cup fresh green beans, cut up, undercooked in salted
    water, or defrosted frozen beans
6 chorizos (Spanish sausages) or sweet fennel Italian
    sausages, skins pierced in several places, simmered in

water 10 minutes, drained, sautéed in olive oil until evenly browned, and cut into ¼-inch-thick slices

16 small fresh shrimp, shells removed, deveined

16 fresh clams or mussels in shells, or 8 of each, scrubbed very clean

8 thin strips pimiento

1 package frozen artichoke hearts, cooked according to package directions, then halved

1. Heat ¼ cup olive oil in the paella pan over medium heat. Season the chicken with salt and pepper and brown it evenly. Remove the chicken and reserve.

2. Pour more oil in the pan, if necessary, and cook the haddock 2 minutes on each side. Remove and reserve.

3. Add a small amount of oil, if necessary, and cook the onion, garlic, and pork over medium heat for 10 minutes, or until the pork is browned. Stir in the tomato, rice, saffron, and chicken broth.

4. Simmer for 10 minutes. Sprinkle the peas, chick-peas, and green beans over the rice. Arrange the chicken, haddock, sausage slices, shrimp, and clams and/or mussels on top of the rice, gently pushing the pieces down into the rice.

5. Bring to a simmer on top of the stove. Then place, covered (a large piece of heavy aluminum foil can be used if you do not have a large enough cover), in a preheated 350 F oven for 15 minutes, or until the rice has absorbed all of the stock and is tender.

6. Garnish the paella with the pimiento strips and artichoke hearts, and return it to the oven for 5 minutes. Let the dish sit out of the oven for 5 minutes, then serve right from the pan, evenly dividing the paella ingredients among your guests.

Serves 8.

Pasta e Fagioli

This meatless dish from Italy was brought to the United States by early immigrants and quickly became an American favorite. Serve with warm Italian garlic bread.

1 pound pea beans, picked over to remove any foreign material
About 3 cups homemade Chicken Broth (page 13), or canned, to cover the beans by 2 inches
1 teaspoon salt
½ teaspoon freshly ground black pepper
2 garlic cloves, peeled and finely chopped
One 1-pound can Italian plum tomatoes, put through a food mill
Leaves from 3 stalks celery
1 carrot, scraped and quartered
1 medium-sized onion, peeled and quartered
1 bay leaf
2 cloves
2 cups ditalini (short, tubular pasta) cooked in boiling, salted water until al dente, and drained
1 cup grated Asiago or Parmesan cheese

1. Soak beans in water to cover for 5 hours; or boil in water for 2 minutes, remove from heat, cover, and soak 1 to 2 hours. Drain.
2. In a large pot, combine the beans, broth, salt, pepper, and garlic. Bring to a boil over medium heat. Reduce heat and simmer for 10 minutes. Stir in the tomatoes.
3. Tie the celery leaves, carrot, onion, bay leaf, and cloves in a piece of cheesecloth. Add it to the pot, cover, and stir occasionally to prevent scorching. Simmer for 1 hour, or until the beans are tender. If liquid cooks off before beans are tender, add more *hot* broth.
4. Remove and discard the cheesecloth bag. Stir in the pasta and

cook, uncovered, until the pasta is just heated through. Taste for seasoning.
5. If the dish is too thick for your taste, add a little chicken stock to obtain the desired consistency.
6. Sprinkle each serving with grated cheese.

Serves 6 to 8.

Peas and Sweetbreads

Peas, probably the most popular of the legumes, and sweetbreads, the most elegant of the variety meats, make a classic and memorable combination. Rice is a good accompaniment.

3 cups fresh shelled peas
6 tablespoons (¾ stick) butter or margarine
3 cups homemade Chicken Broth (page 13), or canned
3 pairs sweetbreads, soaked for 2 or 3 hours in cold water with 1 tablespoon of fresh lemon juice (add ice to the water to keep it cold)
1 teaspoon salt
2 tablespoons freshly squeezed lemon juice
⅔ cup dry white wine (optional)
2 tablespoons flour
Salt and freshly ground black pepper to taste
2 tablespoons chopped fresh parsley

1. Cook the peas in 2 tablespoons butter or margarine and 1 cup chicken broth heated to a simmer, for 15 minutes, or until just tender. Do not overcook.
2. Drain the sweetbreads. Place them in a saucepan; cover with boiling water. Add the salt and lemon juice, and simmer over low heat for 15 minutes.
3. Drain and plunge the sweetbreads into ice water until cool. Drain, then carefully remove and discard all membranes and tubes connecting the lobes. Dry well with paper towels.
4. In a frying pan over medium heat, melt the remaining 4 tablespoons (½ stick) butter or margarine and lightly brown the sweetbreads on both sides. Pour in the wine and simmer until most of the liquid has evaporated. Remove the sweetbreads and keep them warm.
5. Stir the flour into the pan (if necessary add up to 2 tablespoons more butter or margarine to make a smooth paste) and gradu-

ally add the remaining 2 cups broth, a small amount at a time, stirring into a smooth, medium-thick sauce.

6. Lower the heat under the frying pan. Return the sweetbreads to the pan, spooning sauce over them. Cover the pan and simmer for 10 minutes. Do not overcook, or the sweetbreads will toughen. Taste for seasoning, adding salt and pepper if necessary. Stir in the chopped parsley.

7. Serve 1 sweetbread per serving. Spoon a small amount of sauce over each, and surround with peas.

Serves 6.

Red "Chili" Beans with Shrimp and Rice

A favorite in the Southwest, these beans are similar to red kidney beans.

Beans

½ pound dried red beans, picked over to remove any foreign material, boiled in water 2 minutes, removed from heat, covered and soaked 1 to 2 hours and drained
5 cups water
1 medium-sized onion, peeled and chopped
1 garlic clove, peeled and chopped
1 celery stalk, scraped and chopped
½ teaspoon sugar
½ teaspoon salt
¼ teaspoon dried red pepper flakes
20 medium-sized shrimp, peeled, deveined, and cooked about 5 minutes in boiling water to cover (remove shrimp as soon as they turn pink; drain)

1. In a large pot, combine the beans, water, onion, garlic, celery, sugar, salt, and red pepper flakes. Cover pot and bring to a boil. Stir. Reduce heat to low and simmer beans, covered, 1 hour, or until tender but not mushy. Add more *hot* water if necessary.
2. When the beans are almost cooked, mash about 3 or 4 tablespoonfuls against the side of the pot, and stir them back into the pot. This gives the dish a creamy consistency.
3. Stir the precooked shrimp into the bean pot, simmering until warmed through.

Rice

1 cup converted long-grain rice
2½ cups boiling water

1 teaspoon salt
1 tablespoon butter or margarine

1. Stir the rice into the boiling water and add the salt and butter or margarine. Cover, bring to a boil, reduce to a simmer, and cook for 20 minutes.
2. Turn off the heat, leaving the pot covered to keep the rice warm. The rice should also absorb excess moisture. If not, drain.
3. Place a generous serving of hot rice in rimmed soup bowls. Spoon beans and shrimp and the liquid remaining in the pot over the rice.

Serves 4.

Texas Chili con Carne

There are almost as many chili recipes as varieties of beans. We enjoyed this version in San Antonio. For a variation, substitute two 15-ounce cans of lentils or pinto beans for the kidney beans.

- 2 tablespoons olive oil
- 2 medium-sized onions, peeled and chopped
- 1 small green pepper, cored, seeded, and chopped
- 1 small red pepper, cored, seeded, and chopped
- 2 celery stalks, scraped and chopped
- 1 large garlic clove, peeled and minced
- 1 pound ground chuck beef
- 1 level tablespoon chili powder (double it if you prefer more bite)
- ½ teaspoon freshly ground black pepper
- 1 teaspoon salt
- ½ teaspoon cumin, or to taste
- ½ teaspoon celery seeds, crushed
- ½ teaspoon paprika
- 1 teaspoon dried oregano
- One 1-pound can tomatoes
- Two 15-ounce cans red kidney beans, with their liquid

1. In a large pot over medium heat, heat the oil and sauté the onions, peppers, celery, and garlic for 5 minutes, or until the onions are transparent. Do not brown. Add the meat, breaking it up as it cooks and lightly browning it.
2. Stir in the chili powder, black pepper, salt, cumin, celery seeds, paprika, and oregano.
3. Whirl the tomatoes in the blender for 30 seconds, or break them up with your hands. Add them to the pot, stirring in and blending well.
4. Cook over low heat, covered, stirring frequently, for 1 hour.
5. Stir in the beans with their liquid and cook for 30 minutes, stirring frequently to prevent scorching. Taste for seasoning.

Serves 4 to 6.

Cold White Bean Salad and
Hot Lentils with Etienne
Merle's Boned Saddle of Lamb

Etienne Merle makes his magic daily at his restaurant, L'Auberge du Cochon Rouge in Ithaca, New York. He is especially adept at offering legumes in unique, classic ways. Here's one of our favorites. (The lamb is cooked by a simple, effective French method called grilling or pan-broiling, and it should be served rare or medium rare.)

½ recipe cold Cannellini Bean Salad (page 68)
½ lentil preparation from Lentils with Catfish Fillets (page 166)
1 loin of baby lamb, 2½ pounds before boning and trimming (have your butcher trim all connective tissues)
About 2 to 3 tablespoons vegetable oil
Salt and freshly ground black pepper

1. Prepare the beans and lentils, and reserve.
2. Lightly brush the lamb with the vegetable oil and lightly sprinkle with salt and pepper.
3. Place lamb in a large heavy skillet or griddle over high heat for 5 minutes. Turn over and cook 3 minutes (there will be some smoking).
4. Remove lamb promptly and rest in a warm place for 15 minutes before carving, which increases juiciness. Slice the loin saddle at an angle or on the bias, and serve on individual plates, bordered with bean salad and hot lentils.

Note: The lamb can also be cooked on the outdoor grill. First rub the meat all over with oil and season it, then turn over glowing coals, no more than 5 or 6 minutes on each side.

Serves 2 to 4.

Index